How God walked me through lockdown

Writings by a prodigal daughter

A prodigal daughter

Copyright © 2023 A prodigal daughter.

All rights reserved. No part of this book may be used or reproduced by any means, graphic, electronic, or mechanical, including photocopying, recording, taping or by any information storage retrieval system without the written permission of the author except in the case of brief quotations embodied in critical articles and reviews.

WestBow Press books may be ordered through booksellers or by contacting:

WestBow Press
A Division of Thomas Nelson & Zondervan
1663 Liberty Drive
Bloomington, IN 47403
www.westbowpress.com
844-714-3454

Because of the dynamic nature of the Internet, any web addresses or links contained in this book may have changed since publication and may no longer be valid. The views expressed in this work are solely those of the author and do not necessarily reflect the views of the publisher, and the publisher hereby disclaims any responsibility for them.

Any people depicted in stock imagery provided by Getty Images are models, and such images are being used for illustrative purposes only. Certain stock imagery © Getty Images.

Scripture quotations are from the ESV® Bible (The Holy Bible, English Standard Version®), copyright © 2001 by Crossway, a publishing ministry of Good News Publishers. Used by permission. All rights reserved.

Scripture quotations marked (GNT) are from the Good News Translation in Today's English Version- Second Edition Copyright © 1992 by American Bible Society. Used by Permission.

ISBN: 978-1-6642-9072-3 (sc)
ISBN: 978-1-6642-9073-0 (hc)
ISBN: 978-1-6642-9071-6 (e)

Library of Congress Control Number: 2023901639

Print information available on the last page.

WestBow Press rev. date: 03/06/2023

EPIGRAPH

For I know the plans I have for you, declares the Lord, plans for welfare and not for evil, to give you a future and a hope. Then you will call upon me and come and pray to me, and I will hear you. You will seek me and find me, when you seek me with all your heart.

—Jeremiah 29:11–13 (ESV)

I WAITED

I waited a long time for you to return.
I waited and watched and longed for your "Yes."
When you said yes, My heart leapt for joy,
I held My arms open and you ran straight to Me.
Come, my child, let us rejoice,
You have come home to Me, where you belong.
You have forgotten the years you were away from Me.
You see I have melted that time away.
You were always My child and I was always your God.

Contents

Prologue xiii
Introduction xv

Part I Spring 2020 1

Background to the Lockdowns in Ireland, Facing Lockdown,
Jesus as a Servant..1
Lockdown Extended; Isolation; Easter Week.................10
Grieving; The Pure in Heart 16

Part II Summer 2020 19

Jesus and Zacchaeus; A False God.................................19
Weary but a Song of Praise is on My Lips; Challenged by
Confinement...21
The Woman at the Well..24
Some Easing of Restrictions; Jesus: Meek and Humble of Heart.....26
Sunshine in My Soul; Contentedness; Spending Time Wisely 29
God's Perfect Love; the Lord's House............................31
In Stillness; A Call to Trust in Him 32
The Need for God's Healing Touch; Gratitude; My Consolation... 34
Easing of Restrictions; The Land of Shadows; A Call to
Rejoice in Him..36
True Freedom; The Potter's House; Further Easing of Restrictions....39
"A Place at my Table" 42
The Past; Forgiven Much 43
Struggling; Unburdening 45

He is There; Eternal Destination; Just one Sinner; His Suffering 47
Replenished; Old Ways Cast Away 54
Abide in Me; Here I Am 54
God is a Rescuer; The Good Shepherd; His Honoured Guests 56
Where is your Treasure?; "Seek my face" 60
The Meadow; The Prodigal Child 61
Lost Friendship; Distraction; The Lion of Judah; Pride 64
"Be still and know that I am God", Childlike; "Do Not Let
your Heart be Troubled" 67

Part III Autumn 2020 69

God Knows our Thoughts; In the Palm of His Hands;
Living in Limbo 69
Friendship with Jesus; New Restrictions; His Father's House;
A Veil 73
No Losers in God's Eyes; Birthday Party; The Broken Hearted 76
Most Important Thing; The Sea; Division 78
Good News; Old Acquaintances; Passing Through 80
Level 5 Restrictions; Fearless; Setting the Captives Free 82
Drabness; New Garments in Heaven 84

Part IV Winter 2020/2021 85

Restrictions Ahead 85
Jesus: Man of Sorrows; A "Sharp Lockdown" 87
A New Year; House Meetings; Christmas 2020 87
His Healing Hand upon Me; Green Pastures 89
Being His Friend; The Way; My Treasure 90

Part V Spring 2021 93

Springtime; The Best Years; Trusting in Others; Simplicity;
The Best Part of my Day 93

Epilogue 95
Bibliography 97

List of Illustrations

Bird escaping a cage 23
A well..................25
A potter's wheel 41
A Table.................. 42
A Cross 50
Crown of thorns..................52
A Vine..................55
Jesus, the good shepherd 58
Treasure chest 60
Butterflies 62
Lion 66
Squirrel 70
A broken heart 77
Arrow (I am the Way, the Truth and the Life)..................91

Prologue

I am not a theologian or an expert on the Bible. I am just an ordinary person, and this is very much a personal story. I began writing a journal in 2020 when the lockdowns began. I usually wrote during my prayer time. Prayer time is the time I set aside to spend time with God in my room. I focus my mind and heart on Him, though I do think we can pray at any time. A prayer can be as simple as "Thank you God for getting me through the night."

I am a prodigal daughter. I came to know Jesus in a very profound way when I was twenty-one and walked closely with Him until I was twenty-seven. Then, I began to drift farther and farther away to the point where I was leading an immoral and Godless life. I was even at the point where I had no fear of God whatsoever. Still, I couldn't forget His love, which had such a deep impact on me all those years ago. I began the process of returning to Him when I was forty-two.

In 2018, when my health was poor, God drew me into a more intimate walk with Him as I began to spend time in prayer most days. Having the habit of regular prayer time already set up helped me when the lockdowns were imposed in 2020. I do believe that God, in His love, was preparing me for the time that lay ahead, though I didn't know it at the time.

This book is my testimony of how, during the very difficult time of the COVID-19 outbreak and the lockdowns, God gave me a place of rest and filled me with His joy and peace, and He saw me through it all.

Introduction

When I wrote this journal during my prayer time, I wrote down the scriptures I read which resonated the most with how I was feeling that day. Some scriptures were added in later when I decided to write this book. The word of God is as relevant today as it was when it was first written. It is the living word, and it has the power to change your life, if you let it.

I think many people have a misconstrued idea of God in their minds. I know I had before I came to know Him. In these writings, and through the scriptures, I hope you can begin to see God for who He is, and that by having a personal relationship with God, you can begin to live a life that is meaningful and full of hope.

I am speaking of God of the Holy Trinity; the Father, Son, and Holy Spirit are one. Jesus is my God, my true friend, and my constant companion.

It is the Holy Spirit, the living spirit of God, that dwells within me, that has changed my heart and mind over the last number of years. God says that he will give you a heart of love and not of stone.

> And I will give you a new heart, and a new spirit I will put within you. And I will remove the heart of stone from your flesh and give you a heart of flesh. And I will put my Spirit within you, and cause you to walk in my statutes and be careful to obey my rules. (Ezekiel 36:26–27 ESV)

PART I

Spring 2020

Background to the Lockdowns in Ireland, Facing Lockdown, Jesus as a Servant

The first case of the virus in Ireland, a teenaged boy who had traveled from Northern Italy after being on a skiing trip with his school, was diagnosed on the twenty-ninth of February 2020. The boy's school in Dublin closed on the first of March for two weeks.

On the twelfth of March, our Tánaiste (vice president) Leo Varadkar made a State of the Nation Address from Washington, DC. He spoke of the threat posed by the virus and "preparing for all eventualities." He spoke of people dying from the virus, especially older people and people with chronic health conditions. He clarified that the effects of the virus would be mild for the majority of people. He stated that we were in "unchartered territory."

A two-week closure of schools, colleges, and childcare facilities was announced and commenced the following day. Cultural institutions would also be closed. All indoor mass gatherings of more than one hundred people and outdoor mass gatherings of more than five hundred people were canceled. People were to go to work, but, if possible, work from home. Shops would remain open, and plans were put in place to ensure the supply chain would not be interrupted. Restaurants and cafés would stay open and were to look at ways of implementing social distancing and protective measures. People were to reduce their social interactions as much as possible. The public houses were ordered to close on the fifteenth of March.

Tuesday, March 17—St. Patrick's Day

Today is a very quiet day. Usually, people would be out and about attending the parades for St. Patrick's Day, but not this year. I woke up this morning filled with the peace of God. It was quite unexpected! It was as if He had put a blanket of peace over me all day today and it was beautiful.

I am as afraid as the next person right now. Who wouldn't be afraid? I'm not afraid for my own health, but I'm concerned about my elderly relatives and other people close to me.

Saturday, March 21

Lives have been turned upside down by the pandemic. Families have been separated. Fear is alive, and there is an eeriness in the atmosphere. Life is suspended—no birthdays, no christenings, and so forth for the foreseeable future. People feel insecure; it seems like everything is being taken away. In this time, what or who will people turn to?

Personally, my intention is to seek God every day. I am going to keep close contact with family and friends, eat well, rest a lot, and take daily walks. I also plan on continuing to paint and draw, which are hobbies of mine. Overall, I want God to be the centre of my life. I will rely on Him to give me strength of mind, body, and spirit.

In this evening's prayer time, I read this passage.

> Though the fig tree should not blossom, nor fruit be on the vines, the produce of the olive fail and the fields yield no food, the flock be cut off from the fold and there be no herd in the stalls, yet I will rejoice in the Lord; I will take joy in the God of my salvation.
>
> God, the Lord, is my strength; he makes my feet like the deer's; he makes me tread on my high places.
>
> To the choirmaster: with stringed instruments. (Habakkuk 3:17–19)

This scripture is very apt for this time. Even though things seem bleak right now, I can be glad because I know Jesus, and He will give me the strength to get through this time in life. I firmly believe that God will give me strength and that I will experience His joy and peace during this time of adversity.

> In peace I will both lie down and sleep; for you alone, O Lord, make me dwell in safety. (Psalm 4:8)

Sunday, March 22

I'm feeling quite afraid. When I listen to the news and see the images from Northern Italy, this feeling of terror and dread rises up in me. I can't deny that I feel afraid. The Irish media are showing footage from the hospitals in Italy. We see patients in a hospital ward with oxygen helmets over their heads, and they look in bad shape. Sixteen million people in Northern Italy were placed in lockdown on the Ninth of March.

The Holy Spirit whispered this to me today: "Fear not, for I have redeemed you." I know it wasn't a thought or my own voice. When I heard these words, it was like balm for my soul. God does not want me to be afraid.

A prodigal daughter

> You came near when I called on you; you said, "Do not fear!" You have taken up my cause, O Lord; you have redeemed my life. (Lamentations 3:57–58)

Yes, I have been redeemed by Jesus, the Lamb of God, and He has given me a new life. When I came back to Him, I repented and sought His forgiveness. Repentance is a regret and sorrow for what you have done, and it is also a "turning away" from your old way of life. It's a change of direction in how you are going to live and be once you have repented.

This I remembered from when I received God's mercy all those years ago: God will never turn away a contrite heart.

> The sacrifices of God are a broken spirit; a broken and contrite heart, O God, you will not despise. (Psalm 51:17)

The heart of God is to save the lost—"that all should reach repentance."

> The Lord is not slow to fulfil his promise as some count slowness, but is patient towards you, not wishing that any should perish, but that all should reach repentance. (2 Peter 3:9)

Today, I went to the beach with my sister, as I wanted to have a sense of normality and escape what we are facing. It was a beautiful day, and for lots of moments today, the pandemic left my mind, and I experienced joy and peace. I am beginning to rest in the Lord. What a wonderful God I serve!

I am thinking of how patient Jesus is and how He waits for our return. He waited for me so patiently, and He gently called me back to Him. He knocks on the door of the hearts of people and gives an invitation to "recline" at His table. Time is irrelevant to Him. He is meek and humble. When we turn away from Him, we deprive ourselves of so much. Jesus gives you a rich inner life that is worth more than all worldly possessions or wealth; it just doesn't compare. I wouldn't trade my life with Him for anything.

> Behold, I stand at the door and knock. If anyone hears my voice and opens the door, I will come in to him and eat with him, and he with me. (Revelation 3:20)

He will never be outdone in generosity! I think of the miracle of the loaves and fishes. When everyone had their fill of food, there were baskets left over. Jesus was concerned for the welfare of the people who had gathered to hear Him. He didn't want them to be hungry, so He provided food for them to eat.

> Jesus said, "Make the people sit down." Now there was much grass in the place. So the men sat down, about five thousand in number. Jesus then took the loaves, and when he had given thanks, he distributed them to those who were seated. So also the fish, as much as they wanted. And when they had eaten their fill, he told his disciples, "Gather up the leftover fragments, that nothing may be lost." So they gathered them up and filled twelve baskets with fragment from the five barley loaves left by those who had eaten. (John 6:10–13)

Monday, March 23

I know that I am loved by Jesus and that I can put my trust in Him.

> The LORD appeared to him from far away. I have loved you with an everlasting love; therefore I have continued my faithfulness to you. (Jeremiah 31:3)

Here's hoping that life will get back to some normality before the autumn sets in. I started a part-time job in an office at the beginning of March and work from 9:00 a.m. until 3:00 p.m. from Monday to Thursday. I chose to go into the office, having been given the option to work from home. I would prefer to go into work and don't like the idea of working from home at all. I think it would be very isolating. I am not a very disciplined person, and I would struggle with working from home. I would not like my home to become my workplace. The two are then too intertwined. Some people like working from home, but it wouldn't be for me.

The shadow cast by the virus looms like a dark cloud. After spending some time alone with Jesus today, my burden has lightened.

> "Come to me, all who labour and are heavy laden, and I will give you rest. Take my yoke upon you and learn from me, for I am gentle and lowly in heart, and you will find rest for your souls. For my yoke is easy, and my burden is light." (Matthew 11:28–30)

He says to cast our cares unto Him. The same God who walked on the water takes my burdens so that I can be unburdened. How kind He is that He doesn't want His children to be carrying heavy burdens!

Sometimes, I forget that Jesus and the Father are one and that He, Jesus, was there from the beginning of time. How mysterious and magnificent.

> In the beginning was the Word, and the Word was with God, and the Word was God. He was in the beginning with God. All things were made through him, and without him was not anything made that was made. (John 1:1–3)

> And the Word became flesh and dwelt among us, and we have seen his glory, glory as of the only Son from the Father, full of grace and truth. (John 1:14)

Last night, I dreamt that my hair had turned completely grey! In the dream, I kept saying, "I'm too young to be grey." It's such a strange time and I heard on the radio that a lot of people are having very strange dreams. The subconscious mind is always at work.

Wednesday, March 25

I'm thinking that everything in this world passes away and how precarious life can be. The pandemic has stripped people of what is familiar to them. How quickly things can change.

Jesus is giving me joy and peace, especially in this time, and I am so grateful to Him.

He wants us to root our lives in Him and we will remain unshaken, whatever the storm. I don't possess great courage, but He is taking my fear away; in its place, He is giving me a deep joy and peace. I know that without God, I would still be in a state of terror. I feel fear from time to time, but it is not dominating my life as much as it did a few weeks ago.

This is the psalm I read today.

> Hear my cry, O God, listen to my prayer; from the end of the earth I call to you when my heart is faint. Lead me to the rock that is higher than I, for you have been my refuge, a strong tower against the enemy.
>
> Let me dwell in your tent forever! Let me take refuge under the shelter of your wings! (Psalm 61:1–4)
>
> May the Lord give strength to his people! May the Lord bless his people with peace! (Psalm 29:11)

Jesus, I love you so, so much. Thank you from the bottom of my heart. No words can adequately describe my gratitude. Yet again, my cup overflows with God's peace. He is my all.

Saturday, March 28

Ireland went into lockdown last night until the twelfth of April. We are in what is known as Level 5 lockdown, the harshest level of lockdown there is, with Level 1 being the least harsh.

This is a synopsis of the restrictions.

- All non-essential journeys are banned. The only exception to this is that people can travel to work if work is deemed essential and it can't be done from home.
- People can travel beyond two kilometres for the following reasons: shop for food and essential items, attend medical appointments, and visit family for vital reasons such as giving care to the elderly and children.
- People can take brief physical exercise within two kilometres of their homes.
- All public gatherings outside a family household are prohibited.
- More businesses have been ordered to close, such as gyms, retail shops, and sports facilities.
- People over seventy are to "cocoon" and are told to confine themselves to their homes. They are told not to even go out for exercise.

The announcement was a heart-sinking moment and the reality of the situation really hit me, and I am dreading the isolation. I am very daunted by the prospect of living under these restrictions, but I know that God won't abandon me in this time of distress.

I have a choice to make. Do I allow myself to sink into despair or do I lean on God's help and adapt to the situation as best as I can? I'm going to choose the latter. There's always a choice even when it seems like there isn't any. I am choosing to spend time with God and put the effort into my relationship with Him. I opened the Bible to Psalm 63 this evening.

> O God, you are my God and I long for you.
> My whole being desires you; like a dry, worn-out, and waterless land, my soul is thirsty for you.
> Let me see you in the sanctuary; let me see how mighty and glorious you are.
> Your constant love is better than life itself and so I will praise you.
> (Psalm 63:1–3 Good News Translation)

"Let me see you in the sanctuary." Oh Lord, that I may enter into Your sanctuary and find rest. A sanctuary is a place of safety, isn't it? I can go to His sanctuary for some much needed respite in the days and months that lie ahead.

I do feel like a dry, waterless land today. We all have days like these, and God knows we are only human. There are times when I do feel fear, but overall, I feel quite peaceful. It wouldn't be normal to not feel some fear, but the fear isn't overtaking me.

When I came to Him all those years ago, He did not show Himself to me as a royal king of the courts of heaven, though He is that also. Instead, He showed Himself to me as a servant. Jesus, the son of God, served me and His humility was astounding to me. Over time, He brought me to place of wholeness of mind and spirit, and there was a contentedness and a peace in my heart that I have never experienced before. No matter how far away I wandered, the memory of this love and mercy would come back to me.

It was thanks to a friend of mine at that time in my life that I came to faith. My friend and I completed a college course together. Our paths crossed a year or so later and we became good friends. We regularly met and she shared her journey of getting to know Jesus with me and I found it very intriguing. The charismatic movement was very active in Ireland at that time and I attended various meetings that were taking place. I also completed a 'Life in the Spirit' seminar which was life-changing.

While I'm no longer a practicing Catholic, I can testify to the movement of the Holy Spirit within the Catholic community at that time.

Tuesday, March 31

The clocks jumped forward last weekend—it's officially summertime. The birds still sing, the grass still grows, and the daffodils have come up. There are signs of life everywhere despite the current crisis. Life isn't dead.

I've really begun to dread hearing these words: COVID-19, self-isolation, quarantine, sanitize, social distancing. These are words that weren't in our vocabulary a month ago; now they're everywhere.

Lockdown Extended; Isolation; Easter Week

Friday, April 3

I feel so isolated because of the lockdown. I can't begin to describe how isolation feels. It's hard to put it into words. I suppose you could describe it as a deep sense of being alone and feeling lonely—cut off. I miss family and friends. I miss going to my family home that is thirty miles away from where I live.

Do I doubt God? It's so easy to go down the path of moving away from Him. But "Yahweh, I know you are near." I don't want to drift away from Him like I did in the past. Every day there are more deaths. It's all quite horrible. My head actually hurts today. The city is literally like a ghost town and the atmosphere is just dreary and downcast and lifeless. I think to myself that tomorrow will be a better day and next week will be a better week.

Saturday, April 4

The pandemic continues. Spain, Italy, and New York have very high case numbers and deaths. It is easy to get drawn into the news and listening too much seems to exacerbate fear and worry. I need to keep my focus more on the Lord and put my eyes on Him. Oh God, don't let me sink into despair!

During the hour I spent in quiet contemplation today, I felt God's peace permeate my heart and soul. I went down to my room after supper time. It doesn't seem like the natural thing to do: to leave your living room in the evening and spend time with God. It would be easier to sit in front of the television for the rest of the evening, but I decide to make an effort.

God isn't taken by surprise by what is going on but we are. No one saw this coming. Plagues have happened in the past and this too will pass. When it does, I want my relationship with Him to be strong and intact. Maybe I have relied too much on the church services to prop me up spiritually, and now, it's down to me alone and this feels a bit daunting.

This scripture came to my mind at the start of prayer.

> "But seek first the Kingdom of God and his righteousness, and all these things will be added to you. Therefore, do not be anxious about tomorrow, for tomorrow will be anxious for itself. Sufficient for the day is its own trouble." (Matthew 6:33-34)

Jesus is saying to seek Him first, and His righteousness, and everything else will be taken care of. Today has enough worries on its own and there's no need to worry about tomorrow.

I'm not ashamed to say that, at times, I feel overwhelmed at current events. Sometimes, it's as if I "run with fear"—that fear can invade my mind first and then my soul. I believe I have a soul; all humans do. It's what differentiates us from animals. Our souls are what connect us to God and will live forever.

One thing I know: Jesus is my constant companion and my most faithful friend. When I go about my day, He is with me. How can I describe it? It's how you feel when you are in the company of a very dear friend who knows you very, very well.

I love experiencing God's peace and what a wonderful gift it is.

> "I have said these things to you, that in me you may have peace. In the world you will have tribulation. But take heart; I have overcome the world." (John 16:33)

Following God doesn't mean your life is going to be a bed of roses and that life will never be challenging. God didn't promise us a life without trials and troubles. Trials can bring you closer to God or they can drive you away from Him. That is a choice we make: to include Him or exclude Him when we face hard times. When we include Him, He graciously accompanies us.

Thursday, April 9

The lockdown continues. It has been extended until the third of May. That is three weeks longer than anticipated. Also, large gatherings over 5,000 are prohibited until the thirty-first of August. All summer music festivals are going to be cancelled. The death toll is Ireland is 288 out of a population of approximately 4.9 million.

I won't be going to my family home for Easter, which is this coming weekend. I will miss seeing my family, especially my sisters' children who would be visiting over Easter.

I always relax when I'm there as it is a break away from my everyday life. I am finding it difficult to be away for so long. There is a sea view and I miss that view so much! It will be an Easter for reflection and rest.

I feel that God is doing something new in my heart. It's hard to explain, but I feel so strengthened by Him. God says He can make a way in the wilderness and rivers in the desert, and we are in a wilderness and a desert right now.

> Behold, I am doing a new thing; now it springs forth, do you not perceive it? I will make a way in the wilderness and rivers in the desert. (Isaiah 43:19)

This is what I think: God is in charge. Even the seas and mountains obey Him!

> And when he got into the boat, his disciples followed him. And behold, there arose a great storm on the sea, so that the boat was being swamped by the waves; but he was asleep. And they went and woke him, saying, "Save us, Lord; we are perishing." And he said to them, "Why are you afraid, O you of little faith?" Then he rose and rebuked the winds and the sea, and there was a great calm. And the men marvelled, saying, "What sort of man is this, that even winds and sea obey him?" (Matthew 8:23–27)

I find writing very therapeutic and I quite enjoy it. It's just getting my thoughts and feelings out and putting them on a page. I wonder if people are beginning to think about God. Surely some must be. I wonder will people begin to seek God in these times?

April 11 - Easter Saturday

It's been a very, very long day. I have no motivation at all and I am quite fed up. I was in my pyjamas until noon, which is not good. I can't go anywhere or meet anyone. I want to be at my family home and not here, where I live.

I thought of this today. Not even a sparrow falls from the sky without God knowing about it. Isn't that amazing? What is more amazing is that the hairs on your head are numbered. God knows every detail.

> "Are not two sparrows sold for a penny? And not one of them will fall to the ground apart from your Father. But even the hairs of your head are all numbered. Fear not, therefore; you are of more value than many sparrows." (Matthew 10:29–31)

The weather has been lovely today: hazy sunshine for most of the day. I feel sad and downbeat and miss home, family, and friends. I'm finding it hard to put the long weekend down. Time is dragging and this long weekend feels torturous to me.

I'm so glad to be able to go into work for a few hours every day. That's really helping me get through these days. I always think work is a great distraction, whatever the work may be. It could be painting a room or gardening.

I'm not watching more TV than I would usually do. I don't usually watch TV until half past nine at night and turn it off around eleven o'clock. I try to be disciplined in all things as discipline doesn't come naturally to me.

I just finished a book called *Slave*. It's a true story of a young Romanian girl who was trafficked to Ireland and it was a harrowing read. I remember reading *The Diary of Anne Frank* when I was twelve. I prefer biographies to fiction though I have read fiction also down through the years.

April 12—Easter Sunday

I went for a quick cycle this morning. The air was crisp and clear, and a light mist was falling. I woke up feeling pretty tired but I'm feeling the benefit of the cycle now. I had a Zoom call with family today. It feels so strange being separated. Today didn't feel half as long as yesterday, thankfully.

It seems to me that during this crisis, for some their faith will grow and for others, perhaps not. Is this a time in a believer's life where a decision is made to draw closer still or abandon the faith altogether?

There doesn't appear to be any middle ground or time for standing on the fence. It seems that this time is a very definite crossroads.

I have spent time in quiet contemplation today in my room. I don't recite long prayers. I sing, talk to the Lord, and read some scripture, and for the most part, I stay in silence. In that silence, I feel God's presence and His love and peace. Even when I don't feel a whole lot, the important thing is to spend the time and be faithful in that. I want to show Him that I love Him. Isn't loyalty and faithfulness love?

Jesus hears us and knows what is in our hearts. Doesn't the creator of anything have intimate in-depth knowledge of his or her creation? Even when I do a drawing or a painting, I remember the minute details, because I created a finished painting from a blank canvas. It's the same with God. He has in-depth knowledge of all He has created.

I saw lots of birds today, chirping away happily—so innocent and God's creation. I love the sound of birds singing and they sound so happy. I can't help but be a little envious of them. They're completely oblivious to the current situation.

April 13—Easter Monday

The weather was lovely again today: sunny all day though not very warm. I slept on. What's the point in being up and about when we can't go anywhere? We are restricted to a two kilometre travel zone. I find the travel restriction very wearing. I rested for the most part of the day. I do find I'm tired in the mornings and I think it's because of the isolation and restrictions.

I'm beginning to trust God on a deeper level than I had before. I am 100 percent assured of His love and care. I have no doubt at all. He, Jesus, is as real as anyone I know. He's not an illusion. Some people think believing in God is a weakness. I don't.

At a point in my life when I wasn't walking with Him, alcohol became a friend. But this friend will leave you bereft. Drinking would take away all my stress and provide an escape for a short time—a temporary reprieve. I had turned my back on God, and so I was trying to fill that void with alcohol. No matter how hard I tried, I couldn't fill that void.

Grieving; The Pure in Heart

Saturday, April 18

I feel weak today in mind, body, and spirit.

Work is demanding at times as I'm the only administration person in the office,. There is one other person in the office and we have chats every morning which helps to provide a sense of normality. But I am stressed out at the moment, like many people, I'm sure.

> My flesh and my heart may fail, but God is the strength of my heart and my portion forever. (Psalm 73:26)

I think I am in some sort of grief. I'm grieving for my family and friends and for life as it used to be.

I think it's important to be hopeful and God gives me hope. Without Him, I shudder to think how I would be in my head. I believe He is sustaining my sanity. He is my main anchor for sure. He is the bedrock of my life and Jesus knows that I am weak. I'm spending time in prayer every day, though I think I need to give Him more of my time. And what's an hour or hour and a half a day? It's nothing. Here is a scripture that I read today.

> Fear not, for I am with you; be not dismayed, for I am your God; I will strengthen you, I will help you, I will uphold you with my righteous right hand. (Isaiah 41:10)

These words give my heart hope and consolation. Thank you, Lord, for being there for me.

Sunday, April 19

Another weekend is drawing to a close. Overall, it was a good weekend.

I know Jesus is carrying me through this time. I feel so cut off and I don't like that feeling. At times, I feel marooned, isolated, and lonely. One thing I know: the only thing in life that never fades is God, and He is the same today as when He walked the earth. God's light shines in the darkness. He drives away despair and bleakness. I often feel lifted up after spending time with Him.

> Again Jesus spoke to them, saying, "I am the light of the world. Whoever follows me will not walk in darkness, but will have the light of life." (John 8:12)

Praise God for ever and ever, Amen.

Friday, April 24

I have been thinking about television. I find lately that I can't watch anything that has a dark theme running through it as I will have a really bad dream that night. I think God wants our hearts to be pure. The more we watch programmes with dark themes, the more impure our hearts become. It is the difference between a crystal-clear stream and a murky river. You know when a river is clouded, it's really murky underneath and you can't see through it. I want to be more like that crystal clear stream. God put that in my heart today. And I am guilty of watching programmes with dark themes. But I am going to change that from here on in. The beatitudes say that "blessed are the pure in heart, for they shall see God." (Matthew 5:8)

Sunday, April 26

It's hard to know what day it is, or, in fact, what month it is! Another Sunday is upon us—my least favourite day of the week during these times. I feel tired and worn out and could sleep all day. I did an hour's walk yesterday, which I enjoyed, though it was hot. I was thinking that I would rather be anywhere else than where I am now (wishing to be at my family home).

Monday, April 27

I started a painting yesterday so that was positive, and I enjoyed some chocolate. Sunday's low mood carried into today and I woke at 5:35 a.m to the sound of the birds singing so loudly! I am thoroughly fed up as the restrictions are getting to me. If someone asked me how I was today, I would reply "as well as can be in the circumstances."

I still dislike Sunday as I find it's such a long, long day and I struggled to get up out of bed yesterday. I also had a heart flutter; it was high up in my chest and lasted a couple of seconds. Apparently, people are experiencing these at the moment.

PART II

Summer 2020

Jesus and Zacchaeus; A False God

Friday, May 1

One of my favourite Bible stories when I was a child was that of Jesus and Zacchaeus. In the days of Jesus ministry, tax collectors were despised because, firstly, they were collecting taxes for the Roman Empire and secondly, they took more money than they should from people who had very little.

> He entered Jericho and was passing through. And behold, there was a man named Zacchaeus. He was a chief tax collector and was rich. And he was seeking to see who Jesus was, but on account of the crowd he could not, because he was small in stature. So he ran on ahead and climbed up into a sycamore tree to see him, for he was about to pass that way. (Luke 19:1–4)

As Zacchaeus was a chief tax collector, he more than likely went to see Jesus by himself, and possibly would have been keeping his distance from people. It doesn't surprise me that he climbed into a tree as he could remain hidden. Jesus still saw him even though there was a crowd around Him.

Zacchaeus had a curiosity about who Jesus was and his encounter with Him was life changing. He repented and changed his ways.

> So he hurried and came down and received him joyfully. And when they saw it, they all grumbled, "He has gone in to be the guest of a man who is a sinner." And Zacchaeus stood and said to the Lord, "Behold, Lord, half of my goods I give to the poor. And if I have defrauded anyone of anything, I restore it fourfold." And Jesus said to him, "Today salvation has come to this house, since he also is a son of Abraham. For the Son of Man came to seek and to save the lost." (Luke 19:6–10)

Wednesday, May 6

An uneventful day. I'm beginning to experience God's comfort more and more. It is not that I'm not finding this time hard, but I have an inner peace. I know that God has everything under control, and that I am His. I am more sure of God now than I have ever been—sure that He is real and that He is with me.

Yesterday, there was some easing of restrictions. The travel limit is now five kilometres rather than two kilometres. Those who are cocooning can leave their homes for exercise but are to avoid contact with others.

Saturday, May 9

I confess I've been watching too much TV again and I feel pulled away from God. I wonder can TV become a false god? I think it can—if it comes before spending time with Him. No matter what is going on in the world, we, as believers, must strive to have God at the centre of our lives and this can be challenging.

Sunday, May 10

I haven't experienced that low mood today even though it's Sunday. I do have a lightness in my heart and I felt it yesterday evening as well. Thank you, Lord, for lightening my heart!

I can't begin to explain/express how the Lord has comforted me so much over the last number of weeks and how He is consoling me.

> When the cares of my heart are many, your consolations cheer my soul. (Psalm 94:19)

> Trust in the LORD with all your heart, and do not lean on your own understanding. In all your ways acknowledge him, and he will make straight your paths. (Proverbs 3:5–6)

I think this is great advice: to not lean on our own understanding but instead put our trust in God, who understands all.

I did some drawing last night, which was very therapeutic.

Weary but a Song of Praise is on My Lips; Challenged by Confinement

Sunday, May 10

I notice that I'm waking up with a song of praise on my lips every morning. I have begun to listen to worship music very often and I'm singing along to the songs. I feel the companionship of the Saviour for much of my waking day.

God says in the Bible that He will not abandon us and will be with us until the end of time. It's not just my feeling—it's a truth.

> For the LORD will not forsake his people; he will not abandon his heritage. (Psalm 94:14)

A prodigal daughter

Monday, May 11

I slept poorly last night. This seems to be a pattern! I think it's because I find Sunday to be such a long day and being confined to the same place is really quite wearing. Now that it's summertime, I want to be going places.

I went for a quick cycle after work today and the fresh air felt so good. I met a friend during lunch time and the company was welcome. I did some grocery shopping later in the day. There is a sense of tension in the supermarket all the time now. People are on edge and are nervous.

The weeks are beginning to move a bit more quickly than a month ago, thankfully. I'm spending so much time on my own, but I don't feel alone because I know God is with me in my spirit all the time. I don't know what I would do without Him. I think I would be despairing and losing hope.

There seems to be no end in sight to the pandemic, and for the time being, our lives are extremely limited. We now have an understanding of what it is like to live in a society where everyday freedoms are limited or taken away. It hadn't occurred to me up until now.

My sister and I want to go for a drive as we are both hankering to break free from this confinement, even for a little while. While it is not permitted, we feel it is necessary for our sanity.

Tuesday, May 12

I can't get used to living like this. I do notice my mood dips at times and doubt I'm alone in this mood dipping experience. It's a normal reaction to life as it is at the moment.

My prayer is this. Jesus, please give me an abundance of Your peace and hold me upright because I feel I'm falling and I am weak. Carry me, my loving Saviour. Have compassion on me. I love You so much and I know You are with me and that You love me. I humble myself before You and ask that You give me the strength to get through the days and weeks ahead.

> God is our refuge and strength, a very present help in trouble. Therefore we will not fear though the earth gives way, though the mountains be moved into the heart of the sea, though its waters roar and foam, though the mountains tremble at its swelling. (Psalm 46:1–3)

Saturday, May 16

How good it is to spend time in quiet contemplation, and when I do, God grounds me in Him once again.

This time in the world is so difficult and stressful. How I so wish to wake up out of this bad dream and resume normal life!

My sister and I drove to a secluded spot yesterday. We went to a little cove that very few people visit, and it was so good to see the ocean again. The weather was lovely, and we had a picnic there. I cannot begin to express how great it was to have a taste of freedom. It was bliss. It was our first trip anywhere in six weeks. I suddenly became bad humoured when we returned home, and it reminded me of someone letting a bird out of a cage and putting it back in again.

Bird escaping a cage

A prodigal daughter

The Woman at the Well

Saturday, May 16

Now more than ever, we need to put the effort into our relationship with God so that He can strengthen us and "lead us to green pastures." Otherwise, our souls can become barren land. We need to keep going to the source of the life-giving water, which is Christ himself. When Jesus met with the Samaritan woman at the well, He described Himself as "living water." She was alone and drawing water at the hottest time of the day. No one went to the well at that time because of the heat. She must have gone at that time because she was avoiding people.

> Now when Jesus learned that the Pharisees had heard that Jesus was making and baptizing more disciples than John (although Jesus himself did not baptize, but only his disciples), he left Judea and departed again for Galilee. And he had to pass through Samaria. So he came to a town of Samaria called Sychar, near the field that Jacob had given to his son Joseph. Jacob's well was there; so Jesus, wearied as he was from his journey, was sitting beside the well. It was about the sixth hour.
>
> A woman from Samaria came to draw water. Jesus said to her, "Give me a drink." (For his disciples had gone away into the city to buy food.) The Samaritan woman said to him, "How is it that you, a Jew, ask for a drink from me, a woman of Samaria?" (For Jews have no dealings with Samaritans.) Jesus answered her, "If you knew the gift of God, and who it is that is saying to you, 'Give me a drink,' you would have asked him, and he would have given you living water." The woman said to him, "Sir, you have nothing to draw water with, and the well is deep. Where do you

> get that living water? Are you greater than our father Jacob? He gave us the well and drank from it himself, as did his sons and his livestock." Jesus said to her, "Everyone who drinks of this water will be thirsty again, but whoever drinks of the water that I will give him will never be thirsty again. The water that I will give him will become in him a spring of water welling up to eternal life." (John 4:1–14)

That I may keep going to the well! When we come to God, He satisfies our (spiritual) thirst. When I spend time with Him, I feel that spring of water in my soul and spirit and it is satisfying.

A well

Thank you, my dear friend and saviour Jesus–my best friend.

The Holy Spirit revealed something to me about the woman at the well. After her encounter with Jesus, she was no longer ashamed, as she ran back to her people and told them all about Him. She was no longer in hiding.

> So the woman left her water jar and went away into town and said to the people, "Come, see a man who told me all that I ever did. Can this be the Christ?" (John 4:28–29)

I can only conclude that she sought forgiveness and she experienced His love and mercy. This woman was so radically transformed that many in the town believed in Him because of her testimony.

> Many Samaritans from that town believed in him because of the woman's testimony, "He told me all that I ever did." (John 4:39)

Some Easing of Restrictions; Jesus: Meek and Humble of Heart

Monday, May 18

Phase One of the government's "reopening plan" began today. Farmers' markets, garden centres, and other outdoor retail outlets can open as well as outdoor tourism sites. Outdoor fitness activities can resume for individuals and for groups of a maximum of four people. Small groups of up to four people (family or friends) can now meet outdoors within the five kilometre zone.

There is an optimism today which is very welcome. There were more people in town, but people are keeping their distance.

There have been times over the past two months when I have felt such a deep sense of sadness and isolation. Life has lost its colour and its vibrancy.

I notice that time has taken on a different pace and the slower pace is nice. At other times, the time drags and drags.

Without God in my life, I think I would have sunk like a stone. You know, that's what people don't realise: that faith can be a positive aspect of a person's life.

Tuesday, May 19

It's prayer time again, and I've come to look forward to this time I set aside for prayer. I am thinking of these words: "Jesus, remember me when You come into your kingdom" (Luke 23:42).

This is my prayer this evening: Jesus, I pray that I may never become indifferent to Your love. I acknowledge my need of You and I know it is only You who can still my soul in times of trouble.

Your power is immense, and yet, You are gentle.

> You rule the raging of the sea; when its waves rise, you still them. (Psalm 89:9)

> "Take my yoke upon you, and learn from me, for I am gentle and lowly in heart, and you will find rest for your souls." (Matthew 11:29)

You are the only one worthy to open the seals in the Book of Revelation.

> Then I saw in the right hand of him who was seated on the throne a scroll written within and on the back, sealed with seven seals. And I saw a mighty angel proclaiming with a loud voice, "Who is worthy to open the scroll and break its seals?" And no one in heaven or on earth or under the earth was able to open the scroll or to look into it, and I began to weep loudly because no one was found worthy to open the scroll or to look into it. And one of the elders said to me, "Weep no more; behold, the Lion of the tribe of Judah, the Root of David, has conquered, so that he can open the scroll and its seven seals." (Revelation 5:1–5)

You are the lamb of God, a sacrifice for many given of Your own free will. You came to save the lost.

A prodigal daughter

> The next day he saw Jesus coming toward him, and said, "Behold, the Lamb of God, who takes away the sin of the world!" (John 1:29)

> "For the Son of Man came to seek and to save the lost." (Luke 19:10)

Your love breaks through walls that seem impenetrable. You come in gentleness and meekness and never impose Your will. Your love is so great that no human can fathom it. When we take one step towards You, You take ten steps towards us, so eager are You to swoop us up and redeem us into the new life You want us to have with You.

You wash our robes so they are as white as snow. Your love purifies the heart and renews the spirit so that we are new creations—we have been born again.

> Come now, let us reason together, says the LORD: though your sins are like scarlet, they shall be as white as snow; though they are red like crimson, they shall become like wool. (Isaiah 1:18)

You rode into Jerusalem on a donkey, the symbol of humility, and yet You were God.

> And Jesus found a young donkey and sat on it, just as it is written, "Fear not, daughter of Zion; behold, your king is coming, sitting on a donkey's colt!" (John 12:14–15)

You say the greatest amongst us must be the least. In fact, the greatest in Your eyes is the one who serves others as You did.

> "But not so with you. Rather, let the greatest among you become as the youngest, and the leader as one who serves. For who is the greater, one who reclines at

table or one who serves? Is it not the one who reclines at table? But I am among you as the one who serves." (Luke 22:26–27)

When we follow You and put You first, we lose our tendency towards self-absorption and self-centeredness. In so doing, we find life because You give life in abundance. Our lives become more about You and less about ourselves.

Sunshine in My Soul; Contentedness; Spending Time Wisely

Tuesday, May 21

I am off work next week and very glad of the break. It's raining heavily today and it hasn't done so in a while. I was thinking just now that when you have God in your heart, it's like the sun is shining in your being, and today, my soul is dancing!

> Be glad in the LORD, and rejoice, O righteous, and shout for joy, all you upright in heart! (Psalm 32:11)

Thank you, Jesus, for being so loving. You have no idea what a wretched person I am without Him! I am very much at peace. If people only knew how sweet the Lord is and what a true friend He is.

I do think this current crisis really makes celebrity following seem so frivolous and empty. And yet in life today, people are celebrated for all sorts of reasons. It is only the Lord who is worthy of our praise.

> "Worthy are you, our Lord and God, to receive glory and honour and power, for you created all things, and by your will they existed and were created." (Revelation 4:11)

Sunday, May 24

My sister and I made it down to our family home today and had a lovely day. The first thing that struck me when we were near home was the scent of the ocean. It was so salty. This is something I hadn't noticed before. There was such a relief at being home. We had a lovely dinner and then went to the beach and spent an hour there. Bliss!

It is wonderful to be content and I know this contentedness is because of the Lord. I know this because when I didn't walk with Him, I was rarely content. I was continuously running here, there, and everywhere and being oh so busy. It was almost like I couldn't be alone. I couldn't sit with myself. I didn't feel satisfied or fulfilled. Only God can satisfy the deepest part of your being.

> Blessed is the one you choose and bring near, to dwell in your courts! We shall be satisfied with the goodness of your house, the holiness of your temple! (Psalm 65:4)

> "When he calls to me, I will answer him; I will be with him in trouble; I will rescue him and honour him. With long life I will satisfy him and show him my salvation." (Psalm 91:15–16)

God actually renews your youth. In the scriptures, He promises that He is the one

> who satisfies you with good so that your youth is renewed like the eagle's. (Psalm 103:5)

These are a few things I do with my time that I never regret:-

- Spending time with God in quiet contemplation.
- Spending time with family and friends.
- Getting exercise by walking or cycling.
- Reading a good book.

- Listening to good music.
- Going to a beach/enjoying scenery.

I think it's important to spend time wisely. I am guilty of wasting time and this is something I'm actively changing. How we spend our time is something we all have control of, and we make choices every day about how we spend our time.

God's Perfect Love; the Lord's House

Monday, May 25

I had a good day on my first day off. I went for a cycle and had a little bar of chocolate when I reached my destination. I'm learning to enjoy the simple things in a day and trying to uncomplicate my mind. I want to live more in the here and now. The lockdown is teaching me to appreciate the little things in life and not to take them for granted.

It is clear that many people are living in terrible fear and are suffering emotionally.

It is said in the scriptures that perfect love drives out all fear. God's love is a perfect love, and when it fills you, fear begins to dissipate. This is my experience right now. The more time I spend with God, and thinking of Him, the less of a grip fear has on me. Fear is cast out by God's love and it cannot remain where God's love is residing. It's like fire and water—they can't coexist.

> There is no fear in love, but perfect love casts out fear. For fear has to do with punishment, and whoever fears has not been perfected in love. (1 John 4:18)

> For you did not receive the spirit of slavery to fall back into fear, but you have received the Spirit of adoption as sons, by whom we cry, "Abba! Father!" (Romans 8:15)

Isolation is almost as deadly as the virus in the impact it can have. It is said that loneliness can kill, and I believe that is true. I feel for people who are totally isolated, especially the elderly. How sad and difficult it must be for them to be separated from family and friends and from their social activities that gave them something to look forward to every week.

Tuesday, May 26

I read this earlier today and I think it's beautiful.

> One thing have I asked of the LORD, that will I seek after: that I may dwell in the house of the LORD all the days of my life, to gaze upon the beauty of the LORD and to enquire in his temple. (Psalm 27:4)

That I may dwell in the house of the Lord forever!

In Stillness; A Call to Trust in Him

Wednesday, May 27

During prayer time tonight, I realise that it is in stillness and quietness that we can hear the voice of God. Sometimes, there are so many voices that God's voice is drowned out. I heard this in my spirit: "In the stillness, you will hear Me."

> "Be still, and know that I am God. I will be exalted among the nations, I will be exalted in the earth!" (Psalm 46:10)

God is calling us to trust Him completely, especially during these times of uncertainty. I believe it's important to be aware of what is going on in the news, but our main focus should still be on God and on our spiritual lives. If we focus too much on external matters, we lose sight of God.

When my trust begins to wane, I find myself becoming more consumed with what is happening in the news. It is difficult not to be distracted and worry can easily take hold. The only one who has all the answers is God. The more we try to figure things out ourselves, the more muddled we become!

I love the scripture in Matthew's gospel when Jesus talks about worry. He says we cannot add one hour to our lives by worry.

> "Therefore I tell you, do not be anxious about your life, what you will eat or what you will drink, nor about your body, what you will put on. Is not life more than food, and the body more than clothing? Look at the birds of the air: they neither sow nor reap nor gather into barns, and yet your heavenly Father feeds them. Are you not of more value than they? And which of you by being anxious can add a single hour to his span of life? And why are you anxious about clothing? Consider the lilies of the field, how they grow: they neither toil nor spin, yet I tell you, even Solomon in all his glory was not arrayed like one of these. But if God so clothes the grass of the field, which today is alive and tomorrow is thrown into the oven, will he not much more clothe you, O you of little faith? Therefore do not be anxious, saying, 'What shall we eat?' or 'What shall we drink?' or 'What shall we wear?' For the Gentiles seek after all these things, and your heavenly Father knows that you need them all. But seek first the kingdom of God and his righteousness, and all these things will be added to you. Therefore do not be anxious about tomorrow, for tomorrow will be anxious for itself. Sufficient for the day is its own trouble." (Matthew 6:25–34)

This is what I read in the scriptures this evening.

> He provides food for those who fear him; he remembers his covenant forever. (Psalm 111:5)
>
> He sent redemption to his people; he has commanded his covenant forever. Holy and awesome is his name! (Psalm 111:9)

As you can tell, I love the book of Psalms!

Thursday, May 28

I feel hopeful, optimistic, content and at peace. Thank you, heavenly Father, for your loving-kindness towards me. How I want to simplify my walk with Him and be more childlike with Him. Adults overcomplicate everything!

The Need for God's Healing Touch; Gratitude; My Consolation

Saturday, May 30

It's been a very warm, balmy day. Tomorrow is Pentecost Sunday. This is my prayer tonight. God, I need your healing touch in all areas of my life. Father, I pray for an outpouring of your Holy Spirit on me and on all believers and unbelievers. I long for the touch of the Holy Spirit. I long for you, Jesus, more than anything in my life. I long for that union, that intimacy. *Yahweh, I know you are near.* Draw me close to You. I want to draw near to You in everything I do. I want to walk with You. Renew my mind and my spirit.

Sunday, May 31

It's been a beautiful day again. I had a picnic with some friends and we all went to a beach afterwards. All in all, a great day.

I feel a sense of gratitude today for my health and for being able to enjoy a day like today. I'm very thankful to be healthy. I can't tell you how good it feels to be well and content in my soul!

Wednesday June 3

Today, I don't feel God's presence, but faith is not a feeling, and it doesn't mean He loves me any less than He did yesterday. He is unwavering in His love towards me.

> But you, O Lord, are a God merciful and gracious, slow to anger and abounding in steadfast love and faithfulness. (Psalm 86:15)

Isn't life so fleeting? These writings from the book of Isaiah describe what I'm thinking. Only God remains forever.

> A voice says, "Cry!" And I said, "What shall I cry?" All flesh is grass, and all its beauty is like the flower of the field. The grass withers, the flower fades when the breath of the Lord blows on it; surely the people are grass. The grass withers, the flower fades, but the word of our God will stand forever. (Isaiah 40:6–8)

Friday, June 5

A lot of people over the age of seventy haven't had any proper contact in ten weeks. There is no life that hasn't been affected by the pandemic and the lockdowns. What about the women and children who are trapped in the situation of domestic violence? Their lives right now must be a never-ending nightmare. It will be difficult to quantify the collateral damage caused by the lockdowns.

In prayer time, the Holy Spirit consoles me as only the Holy Spirit can. Thank you, Holy Spirit. I don't claim to understand the Holy Trinity, but I recognise the Holy Spirit. He is so gentle, and yet, so powerful.

Saturday, June 6

It has been a windy and mostly sunny day. I don't have much to say today. My sister and I are going home tomorrow and are looking forward to it very much.

Sunday, June 7

We had a lovely day at home and spent some time at the beach.

Monday, June 8

It's difficult to escape the coronavirus crisis. Everywhere you go, there are the big yellow posters that we've all become so familiar with telling us to wash our hands and keep two metres apart. Now, there is mention of the second wave on the media.

If I didn't have my faith, I don't know how I would navigate these days. I really don't.

Easing of Restrictions; The Land of Shadows; A Call to Rejoice in Him

Monday, June 8

We are now in Phase Two of the government's reopening plan. We can now travel within our own county, and up to twenty kilometres, if crossing county boundaries. We can meet up to six people from outside our own households (indoor and outdoor) for social gatherings organised outdoor exercise, sporting, cultural, or social activities of up to fifteen people can now take place. Most shops are opening with shopping centres to open on the fifteenth of June. Outdoor children's summer camps will operate. We should still work from home, if possible. People over seventy and the medically vulnerable can now have small numbers of people in their homes.

Tuesday, June 9

I had such a lovely day at home on Sunday, and now I'm back to feeling isolated again and I am downcast. Time moved very slowly at work. Usually, I would make arrangements to meet friends for lunch once or twice a week, which always gives my working day a boost. This is not possible now, and this adds to the isolation.

In prayer time this evening, I heard these words in my spirit: "Rejoice in your God."

> May all who seek you rejoice and be glad in you! May those who love your salvation say evermore, "God is great!" (Psalm 70:4)

I was downcast all day, and now I am joyful and lifted up. Thank you, Jesus, for lifting me up again. Your goodness amazes and humbles me.

> He put a new song in my mouth, a song of praise to our God. Many will see and fear, and put their trust in the LORD. (Psalm 40:3)

> Rejoice in the Lord always; again I will say, rejoice. (Philippians 4:4)

I read this passage from the Book of Isaiah.

> The people who walked in darkness have seen a great light; those who dwelt in a land of deep darkness, on them has light shone. (Isaiah 9:2)

I like this translation from the Good News Bible.

> The people who walked in darkness have seen a great light. They lived in a land of shadows, but now light is shining on them. You have given them great joy, Lord;

> you have made them happy. They rejoice in what you have done, as people rejoice when they harvest grain or when they divide captured wealth. For you have broken the yoke that burdened them and the rod that beat their shoulders. (Isaiah 9:2–4 GNT)

They lived in a "land of shadows." When God is absent from our lives, we can find ourselves living in a land of shadows. We can get used to living in the shadows, and it's only when God's light shines on us that we realise we were in the shade all along.

In this trying time in life, God still calls us to rejoice in Him. When we rejoice in Him, He lifts us out of the shadows. How great a God He is that He gives us such joy and peace. This joy is an expression of His love, as is His mercy and healing. They all flow from His love.

The love of God is like a waterfall that never stops flowing!

I feel the inner desire to write about what God is doing for me and He truly is the God of my very ordinary every day.

I think that mostly, I'm glimpsing Him. Then, there are the moments in time when He draws very close and reveals Himself to me. I'm reminded by the prophet Jeremiah that God already knows me very well and He even knew me before I was born. It's hard to wrap my head around that! These words were spoken to him.

> "Before I formed you in the womb I knew you, and before you were born I consecrated you; I appointed you a prophet to the nations." (Jeremiah 1:5)

Friday, June 12

Today, I feel rested. I woke again this morning with a song of praise on my lips. This is what I read in the scriptures this evening and I love this psalm.

Oh come, let us sing to the LORD;
let us make a joyful noise to the rock of our salvation!
Let us come into his presence with thanksgiving;
Let us make a joyful noise to him with songs of praise!
For the LORD is a great God, and a great King above all gods.
In his hand are the depths of the earth; the heights of the mountains are his also.
The sea is his, for he made it, and his hands formed the dry land.
Oh come, let us worship and bow down; let us kneel before the LORD, our Maker!
For he is our God, and we are the people of his pasture, and the sheep of his hand. (Psalm 95:1–7)

True Freedom; The Potter's House; Further Easing of Restrictions

Monday, June 15

There are more people in town today, following the opening of shops, which is great to see.

I was singing songs of praise on the cycle to work and on the way home, and felt as free a bird! It is true that only Jesus can give you true freedom and what a wonderful freedom it is.

> "So if the Son sets you free, you will be free indeed."
> (John 8:36)

When I was living life according to my own desires and wants, and doing as I pleased, I thought I was free, but I wasn't. I was the opposite of free.

> Jesus answered them, "Truly, truly, I say to you, everyone who practises sin is a slave to sin."(John 8:34)

A prodigal daughter

I used to live life according to the flesh and it didn't bring me peace or freedom. This scripture explains this perfectly.

> For those who live according to the flesh set their minds on the things of the flesh, but those who live according to the Spirit set their minds on the things of the Spirit. For to set the mind on the flesh is death, but to set the mind on the Spirit is life and peace. (Romans 8:5–6)

Not living life according to God's ways has consequences both spiritually and emotionally. I could have avoided a lot of pain and heartache if I had been living life "according to the Spirit" and not "according to the flesh."

I made many bad choices and regretted a lot of my actions. I was full of pride, self-justification, and I was very self-centred. I looked for peace and happiness in all the wrong places and lived a very hectic life. I did not think that rest was important.

I thought of this recently. When you submit to God, He shines a light on all the dark places in you, and on the parts of you that are not pleasing to Him. You begin to see what needs to change in your life; it is His grace and healing touch that make those changes possible. I always say, "I am a work in progress!" In the book of Jeremiah, God describes Himself as a potter.

> The word that came to Jeremiah from the LORD: "Arise, and go down to the potter's house, and there I will let you hear my words." So I went down to the potter's house, and there he was working at his wheel. And the vessel he was making of clay was spoiled in the potter's hand, and he reworked it into another vessel, as it seemed good to the potter to do. Then the word of the LORD came to me: "O house of Israel, can

I not do with you as this potter has done? declares the
LORD. Behold, like the clay in the potter's hand, so are
you in my hand, O house of Israel. (Jeremiah 18:1–6)

A potter's wheel

Can we humble ourselves enough to be like clay in the hands of the master potter? As He is the master potter, He can create something beautiful out of something broken and make beauty from ashes.

> to grant to those who mourn in Zion—to give them a beautiful headdress instead of ashes, the oil of gladness instead of mourning, the garment of praise instead of a faint spirit. (Isaiah 61:3)

We are moving to Phase Three of the opening plan. The following will be opening on June 29: all remaining businesses (that didn't open on June 8), amenities and workplaces; adult education facilities; pre-schools, crèches, summer camps and youth clubs; hairdressers and beauty salons; places of worship; museums, galleries, theatres and cinemas, cafés, restaurants, hotels, and holidays parks. Fifty people can gather indoors and 200 outdoors.

When everything is shut, there seems little point in arranging to meet anyone as there is nowhere to go. I'm looking forward to the twenty-ninth of June. It seems ages away but it's only two weeks.

My job is finishing up this week. I'm not that surprised, as there has been an inevitable downturn in business.

I'm not looking forward to being off work. For me, one of the hardest things about not having a job is the uncertainty that goes with it. How long will I be out of work? How hard will it be to get a job? How will I spend the time? Will I be able to keep my head above water and not run into debt?

"A Place at my Table"

Friday, June 19

When I was in prayer just now, I heard these words in my spirit: "You have a place at my table." I have no words to express how touched I am at these words.

> You prepare a table before me in the presence of my enemies; you anoint my head with oil; my cup overflows. (Psalm 23:5)

A Table

The Past; Forgiven Much

Monday, June 22

This is my first week of unemployment. It is what it is. I'm just going to take one day at a time. I will try to have some sort of a routine every day.

Monday, June 29

Today, I went on a long walk and enjoyed every minute of it. Despite my circumstances, there is a joy in my heart.

Tuesday, June 30

A busy day. I painted a room and I'm very happy with how it has turned out. I have a great sense of satisfaction.

I find that going to my room for prayer time has now become like second nature and I rarely miss a day. It has become something I now *want* to do.

I have found recently that I'm not bound by my past anymore. It is like a load has been lifted from my shoulders. I know this is the work of God. Thank you, my sweet Jesus and my dear friend, for loosening the hold the past had on me. He doesn't remind me of my past sins because when He forgives, He forgets. I have to remind myself of that every now and again. When my old ways of living come to the forefront of my mind, I say, "It's okay. God doesn't remember them anymore and they've been washed away."

> I, I am he who blots out your transgressions for my own sake, and I will not remember your sins. (Isaiah 43:25)
>
> Remember not the former things, nor consider the things of old. (Isaiah 43:18)

A prodigal daughter

I think of the woman with the expensive jar of alabaster oil who went to Simon the Pharisee's house when she learned Jesus was going to be there. She threw herself down at His feet in a gesture of faith, humility, and repentance. She was seeking His mercy and received it in abundance.

> One of the Pharisees asked him to eat with him, and he went into the Pharisee's house and reclined at table. And behold, a woman of the city, who was a sinner, when she learned that he was reclining at table in the Pharisee's house, brought an alabaster flask of ointment, and standing behind him at his feet, weeping, she began to wet his feet with her tears and wiped them with the hair of her head and kissed his feet and anointed them with the ointment. Now when the Pharisee who had invited him saw this, he said to himself, "If this man were a prophet, he would have known who and what sort of woman this is who is touching him, for she is a sinner. And Jesus answering said to him, "Simon, I have something to say to you." And he answered, "Say it, Teacher."
>
> "A certain money-lender had two debtors. One owed five hundred denarii, and the other fifty. When they could not pay, he cancelled the debt of both. Now which of them will love him more?" Simon answered, "The one, I suppose, for whom he cancelled the larger debt." And he said to him, "You have judged rightly." Then turning towards the woman he said to Simon, "Do you see this woman? I entered your house; you gave me no water for my feet, but she has wet my feet with her tears and wiped them with her hair. You gave me no kiss, but from the time I came in she has not ceased to kiss my feet. You did not anoint my head with oil, but she has anointed my feet with ointment.

Therefore I tell you, her sins, which are many, are forgiven—for she loved much. But he who is forgiven little, loves little." And he said to her, "Your sins are forgiven." Then those who were at table with him began to say among themselves, "Who is this, who even forgives sins?" And he said to the woman, "Your faith has saved you; go in peace." (Luke 7:36–50)

Imagine how grateful you would be if someone agreed to pay a debt for you? Imagine how much more grateful you would be if it was a large debt?

I have been forgiven much and for that I am forever grateful. Thank you, Jesus, for forgiving me of so much. I pray that I may never take your mercy for granted.

Struggling; Unburdening

Wednesday, July 1

All churches are still closed and I'm really missing the collective experience of worship and fellowship.

I met with two of my long-term friends for lunch today. It was great to be together and catch up. They are both important to me and I value their friendship greatly. We've known one another for over twenty years.

I find the days are going by nicely, not too fast and not too slow, and I try to take each day at a time.

This is my prayer every morning: Lord Jesus, thank you that I am alive today and can open my eyes. Thank you for bringing me safely through the night. I give my heart and myself to you today. I am yours. I need Your love, Your friendship, and Your grace. When I feel deserted, I know that You are with me. When I feel alone, despondent and when I'm weak, You are there right by my side, forever faithful.

Thursday, July 2

I woke up with a heaviness in my head after having a really bad dream. My mood is flat, and I've been frustrated and irritable all day. I still have a slight headache. I suppose days like these are inevitable in the current situation.

When I came to prayer in the late evening, I realised I didn't invite God into my day and didn't even acknowledge Him all day. I said this to Him: "Jesus, can I lean on Your shoulder and rest myself because I am weary to the bone?" I sat in silence, and I began to feel His peace. The heaviness left me, and He renewed my strength.

> But they who wait for the LORD shall renew their strength; they shall mount up with wings like eagles; they shall run and not be weary; they shall walk and not faint. (Isaiah 40:31)

It's so easy to say, "I had a bad day because of x, y, or z," when often, we have bad days because we decide to carry our burdens all by ourselves rather than unburdening ourselves to God.

Is there a part of us that doesn't want to burden Him? The scriptures say we can lay our worries down at His feet and that He is with us in our trouble and strife.

> Humble yourselves, therefore, under the mighty hand of God so that at the proper time he may exalt you, casting all your anxieties on him, because he cares for you. (1 Peter 5:7)

> When you pass through the waters, I will be with you; and through the rivers, they shall not overwhelm you;

> when you walk through fire you shall not be burned, and the flame shall not consume you. (Isaiah 43:2)
>
> Cast your burden on the LORD, and he will sustain you; he will never permit the righteous to be moved. (Psalm 55:22)

Jesus, I ask for Your peace in my soul and I feel it now, permeating my heart and soul. "Amazing grace, how sweet the sound, that saved a wretch like me."

He is There; Eternal Destination; Just one Sinner; His Suffering

Friday, July 3

Morning time: I woke this morning filled with peace. My mind is completely at peace and I have a stillness in my being. I feel so loved by God this morning.

> "Peace I leave with you; my peace I give to you. Not as the world gives do I give to you. Let not your hearts be troubled, neither let them be afraid." (John 14:27)

Thank you, my loving Saviour, for giving me Your peace. You never cease to love me or listen to my prayer.

Evening time: When times are hard, Jesus is there. When friends are busy and you lack companionship, He is your best friend and He stays closer to you than a brother.

> A man of many companions may come to ruin, but there is a friend who sticks closer than a brother. (Proverbs 18:24)

I just opened the Bible at this psalm.

> The Lord is the strength of his people; he is the saving refuge of his anointed. Oh, save your people and bless your heritage! Be their shepherd and carry them forever. (Psalm 28:8–9)

There have been times over the past few months when it has seemed as if I was being carried.

> Even to your old age I am he, and to grey hairs I will carry you. I have made, and I will bear; I will carry and will save. (Isaiah 46:4)

When we are in our eternal home in heaven, we will never shed a tear again or be lonely or sad.

> He will wipe away every tear from their eyes, and death shall be no more, neither shall there be mourning, nor crying, nor pain anymore, for the former things have passed away. (Revelation 21:4)

The opposite of heaven is hell: a place of weeping, of torment, of darkness, and of total separation from God—forever. There is no redemption to be had once you reach there.

> "In that place there will be weeping and gnashing of teeth, when you see Abraham and Isaac and Jacob and all the prophets in the kingdom of God but you yourselves cast out." (Luke 13:28)

> "For what does it profit a man to gain the whole world and forfeit his soul? For what can a man give in return for his soul?" (Mark 8:36–37)

> "And do not fear those who kill the body but cannot kill the soul. Rather fear him who can destroy both soul and body in hell." (Matthew 10:28)

It is not popular to speak of hell and it seems to be rarely spoken of now. However, Jesus spoke of hell many times during His ministry. Do we not warn of danger out of love? He spoke of it in the parable of the rich man and Lazarus.

> "There was a rich man who was clothed in purple and fine linen and who feasted sumptuously every day. And at his gate was laid a poor man named Lazarus, covered with sores, who desired to be fed with what fell from the rich man's table. Moreover, even the dogs came and licked his sores. The poor man died and was carried by the angels to Abraham's side. The rich man also died and was buried, and in Hades, being in torment, he lifted up his eyes and saw Abraham far off and Lazarus at his side. And he called out, 'Father Abraham, have mercy on me, and send Lazarus to dip the end of his finger in water and cool my tongue, for I am in anguish in this flame.' But Abraham said, 'Child, remember that you in your lifetime received your good things, and Lazarus in like manner bad things; but now he is comforted here, and you are in anguish. And besides all this, between us and you a great chasm has been fixed, in order that those who would pass from here to you may not be able, and none may cross from there to us.' And he said, 'Then I beg you, father, to send him to my father's house—for I have five brothers—so that he may warn them, lest they also come into this place of torment.' But Abraham said, 'They have Moses and the Prophets; let them hear them.' And he said, 'No, father Abraham, but if someone goes to them from the dead, they will repent.' He said to him, 'If they do not hear Moses and the Prophets, neither will they be convinced if someone should rise from the dead.'" (Luke 16:19–31)

I know for certain my destination was hell had I not repented, and this would have been just. I pray for the lost all of the time, especially for those who have no one to pray for them. I was once lost and maybe it was someone's prayers for me that brought me back and saved me from that fate.

There is much rejoicing in heaven when one sinner repents. Heaven throws a party! There are trumpets blowing, harps being played, and angels singing, and once again, the Lamb of God has the victory. Heaven rejoices because Jesus's death was not in vain.

> "Just so, I tell you, there is joy before the angels of God over one sinner who repents." (Luke 15:10)

Did you notice how Jesus says "one sinner"? Just one sinner is important to Him. Just one.

Not long ago, I watched a YouTube video entitled "The Crucifixion: A Medical Perspective." This video brought me a greater understanding of what He suffered and it is well worth watching.[1]

A Cross

---
[1] Central Christian Church, "The Crucifixion: A Medical Perspective," YouTube video, 28 March 2008, https://www.youtube.com/watch?v=T-EVfxABSoU.

The apostle Luke said He sweated blood in the Garden of Gethsemane.

> And being in agony he prayed more earnestly; and his sweat became like great drops of blood falling down to the ground. (Luke 22:44)

Hematidrosis is the medical term for sweating blood, which is a rare condition and "is said to occur when a person is facing death or other extremely stressful events."[2]

The guards mocked Him as they beat Him and blasphemed against Him.

> Now the men who were holding Jesus in custody were mocking him as they beat him. (Luke 22:63)

> And they said many other things against him, blaspheming him. (Luke 22:65)

Then, the Roman soldiers flogged Him from His shoulders to legs with a whip known as the cat o' nine tails. The whip was actually several whips tied together at the handle. The whipping was so severe in those times that pieces of muscle would come out through the skin because each tassel had sharp bones and pieces of metal attached onto it. He would have received at least thirty-nine lashes.

They placed a crown of thorns on His head in a gesture of mockery. The thorns would have been two to five inches long. The crown wasn't just placed on His head, rather it was beaten onto His head with a rod.

---

[2] "Hematidrosis," *Segen's Medical Dictionary*, accessed 19 October 2022, https://medical-dictionary.thefreedictionary.com/hematidrosis.

Crown of thorns

> And they clothed him in a purple cloak, and twisting together a crown of thorns, they put it on him. (Mark 15:17)

He was made to carry the cross all the way up the hill while the baying crowd, except for His faithful followers, mocked and jeered Him. Any human man would not have been able to endure what He endured.

It is thought now that the nails were hammered into the wrists so His body would not fall forward while hanging on the cross.

The Romans had perfected the act of crucifixion so that there was maximum pain with minimum blood loss. They knew exactly where to put the nails in the wrists so they would miss the arteries. The nails would have hit the median nerve and caused shock sensations.

Experts say the nails were hammered into the shins. Shin bones with nail fragments from crucifixions have been found which support this hypothesis.

What must have made Him finish the journey up to the hill of Golgotha? It was His love and the thought of just 'one sinner' being redeemed. His last words were, "It is finished."

> When Jesus had received the sour wine, he said, "It is finished," and he bowed his head and gave up his spirit. (John 19:30)

Victims of crucifixions could survive for up to six days. While on the cross, victims had to push themselves up to be able to take in a breath. Once their legs were broken, pushing up was no longer possible and they would die of suffocation very quickly. This is why the soldiers came to break His legs.

Now, I understand why Jesus said this.

> "No one takes it from me, but I lay it down of my own accord. I have authority to lay it down, and I have authority to take it up again. This charge I have received from my Father." (John 10:18)

He laid down His life of His own accord. There is no greater love than this.

> "Greater love has no one than this, that someone lay down his life for his friends." (John 15:13)

The scriptures say that not a bone in His body would be broken.

> He keeps all his bones; not one of them is broken. (Psalm 34:20)

> For these things took place that the Scripture might be fulfilled: "Not one of his bones will be broken." (John 19:36)

It is hard to fathom how horrific it was for Him. There is a song called "Scars in Heaven" that says the only wounds in heaven are the wounds on the hands and feet of Jesus.

Replenished; Old Ways Cast Away

Sunday, July 5

I had a lovely weekend at my family home. I went for a walk along the beach in the morning and it was very enjoyable. I just feel so content and joyful. I actually feel twenty years younger than I am! It says in the scriptures that God refreshes His people. It is true and that is exactly what He has done for me. Thank you, Jesus, my majesty and the King of Kings!

> "For I will satisfy the weary soul, and every languishing soul I will replenish." (Jeremiah 31:25)

When we come to know Christ, He makes us new creations and the old ways are cast away. It is almost like we are given new sets of clothes and we go from rags to riches.

> Therefore, if anyone is in Christ, he is a new creation. The old has passed away; behold, the new has come. All this is from God, who through Christ reconciled us to himself and gave us the ministry of reconciliation; that is, in Christ God was reconciling the world to himself, not counting their trespasses against them, and entrusting to us the message of reconciliation. (2 Corinthians 5:17–19)

Abide in Me; Here I Am

Friday, July 10

I went to a park yesterday with a small group of cyclists I cycle with from time to time. I really enjoyed the cycle and being in the company of others. I woke up this morning thinking of this: "Abide in Me."

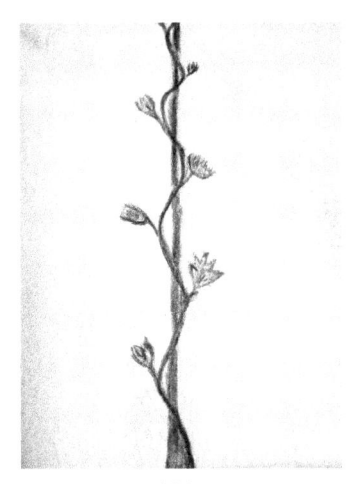

A Vine

"Abide in me, and I in you. As the branch cannot bear fruit by itself, unless it abides in the vine, neither can you, unless you abide in me. I am the vine; you are the branches. Whoever abides in me and I in him, he it is that bears much fruit, for apart from me you can do nothing." (John 15:4–5)

Jesus makes it clear that to bear fruit, the branches must stay connected to the vine. You could say that the vine is the life source for the branches, just in the same way that Jesus is our life source, and we are to stay attached to Him. He wants us to root our lives in Him. I love trees and often marvel at the magnificence of the roots that are visible. I wonder how far below the earth do the invisible roots go? The farther down the roots are, the stronger the tree. In the same way, the stronger our roots are in God, the less likely we are to be shaken by trials and adversities.

One of the girls in the cycling group was saying that she is working from home and I could tell she finds it lonely. Her usual sparkle was missing. It struck me that there are many people now living very isolated lives and it must be so difficult. It must be hard on single people and I'm sure it's pretty stressful for families too.

Here is tonight's psalm.

> May all who come to you be glad and joyful. May all who are thankful for your salvation always say "How great is God!" I am weak and poor; come to me quickly O God —hurry to my aid! (Psalm 70:4–5, GNT)

I was humming this while I was cycling earlier this week: I rest in You. When the storm was raging all around, I turn to you. And now I stand on solid ground. You put me safe upon a rock and gave me shelter underneath your wings.

There are often times when I wonder if I disappoint God. Do I do what He asks of me? Do I even know when He is asking me to do or say something? All I can do is show my loyalty to Him by spending time with Him every day. I show my love for Him by showing kindness to everyone as much as I can. If we could only see people through God's eyes! I try every day to have a good attitude. I try to imitate Him. Often, I fail dismally, yet I still remember He loves me.

I suppose all I can say to Him is "Lord, I am willing to do as you ask of me but I need Your help. I need to know what You want me to do. Who should I talk to about You? Guide me. And I am willing. I want to be obedient and loyal and faithful to You." What I can do is make the daily effort (for want of a better word) to walk with Him and so, I lay my life before Him and He will do the rest.

God is a Rescuer; The Good Shepherd; His Honoured Guests

Sunday, July 12

It was a good day. I went to a beach with my sister for a couple of hours. It was cloudy and breezy but it was still lovely to get the fresh air.

The current situation we find ourselves in can be overwhelming at times and so many people must be experiencing loneliness right now. Loneliness leads to despair, and sometimes, it's hard to come back from a place of despair. But God is a rescuer.

> "But now I will come," says the Lord "because the needy are oppressed and the persecuted groan in pain. I will give them the security they long for." The promises of the Lord can be trusted; they are as genuine as silver refined seven times in the furnace. (Psalm 12:5–6, GNT)

> "Rescue the weak and the needy; deliver them from the hand of the wicked." (Psalm 82:4)

I'm beginning to feel very secure because I know that God is with me and that He won't let me down. He is truly my sanctuary in these days, for which I will be forever thankful. I am as surefooted as a deer on a high mountain top! I am sure I won't fall.

> He made my feet like the feet of a deer and set me secure on the heights. (2 Samuel 22:34)

Thank you, Lord, for Your constant love. My heart is Yours.

Monday, July 13

A good day. Did you ever have a dream that you didn't want to leave? I woke up wanting to stay in my dream, but it evaporated soon after I woke.

I spent some time with a friend today. I value friendship highly. I need company sometimes, that's for sure. My sister is a lot more sociable than me. She talks to everyone and people like her instantly. I'm the opposite. It takes time to get to know me and I don't give my trust easily.

A prodigal daughter

I do feel a little lost without a job but I'm keeping a routine as best as I can.

I read in the headlines today that there is an increase of twenty percent in the amount of people who are looking for help with their mental health. It was said that people are suffering from clinical depression and they're convinced they're going to contract the virus. That's very sad and there isn't a quick fix for depression. It can be a long road back to full health. Mental health can be like a seesaw. I have had fluctuations in my mood as a result of the situation we are living in, but it hasn't been a catastrophic fluctuation.

Tuesday, July 14

I do not fear today nor do I fear tomorrow—my life is in God's hands. Jesus said that He is the good shepherd and is always taking care of His flock. What a good shepherd He is! Yahweh, I know you are near.

Jesus, the good shepherd

Thursday, July 16

Today, I went for a cycle with my cycling group and enjoyed it very much. I opened the Bible at Psalm 23 this evening: the Good Shepherd.

> The LORD is my shepherd; I have everything I need.
> He lets me rest in fields of green grass and leads me to quiet pools of fresh water.
> He gives me new strength.
> He guides me in the right paths, as he has promised.
> Even if I go through the deepest darkness, I will not be afraid, LORD, for you are with me.
> Your shepherd's rod and staff protect me.
> You prepare a banquet for me, where all my enemies can see me; you welcome me as an honoured guest and fill my cup to the brim.
> I know that your goodness and love will be with me all my life; and your house will be my home as long as I live. (Psalm 23: 1—6, GNT)

You welcome me as an honoured guest and fill my cup to the brim.

The world may scoff at the believer, but to Jesus, we are His honoured guests and He prepares a banquet for us. It's a banquet because when we dine with Him, we will be in His kingdom. When I imagine this banquet, I see a beautifully adorned table draped in purple velvet. The chairs are beautiful with detailed ornamental carvings. There are no half measures! Our cups are filled to the brims.

God calls us to be humble in this life. Believers may well be overlooked while on the earth, but in heaven, we are the honoured guests of the King of Kings and the Lord of Lords.

I was thinking today of how reliable the Lord is. Friends can bail on you and family have their own lives going on, but God is always with His children. He is faithful and true to His word.

> The steadfast love of the LORD never ceases, his mercies never come to an end; they are new every morning; great is your faithfulness. (Lamentations 3: 22–23)

Where is your Treasure?; "Seek my face"

Friday, July 17

Any time spent with the Lord is a storing up of treasure you will find when you enter the Kingdom of God (Heaven). The beauty of this treasure is that it will never fade. You see, everything that people hold up as treasure in this life eventually rusts and gathers dust.

> "Do not lay up for yourselves treasures on earth, where moth and rust destroy and where thieves break in and steal, but lay up for yourselves treasures in heaven, where neither moth nor rust destroys and where thieves do not break in and steal." (Matthew 6:19–20)

Treasure chest

Jesus is the ultimate treasure and when you find Him, you will begin to understand what true treasure is.

Oh Lord Jesus, I need you so much. Thank you, my loving Jesus—always at my side.

I heard this in my spirit today: "Seek my face."

> You have said, "Seek my face." My heart says to you, "Your face, LORD, do I seek." (Psalm 27:8)

And who am I, that Jesus, true God and true man, should shine His face on me? I pray that I may never take Him for granted.

The Meadow; The Prodigal Child

Sunday, July 19

My sister and I visited our family home on Saturday. We got a flat tyre about twenty minutes into the journey. I was telephoning the rescue service when a car pulled up beside us and a gentleman offered to help us. He was very pleasant and changed the tyre with no fuss. I followed him to a nearby tyre shop and got it fixed. It still amazes me how well God looks after me. Thank you, Lord, for sending this man our way.

While at my family home, I went for a walk to a secluded spot for some quiet time as I wanted to be alone with God, just He and I. It's a small piece of land that is not being used anymore and so the ground has had time to flourish into a meadow.

I sat on the railing and listened to the sounds of the birds singing and watched the butterflies flying around in the tall grass. Isn't God's creation so beautiful?

Butterflies

I chatted to the Lord, and it was so good to be able to enjoy the stillness of the moment with Him and to feel His nearness. The sun was out, and it was so warm. I slept really well, as I usually do when I'm at my family home. It's in the countryside and very little traffic passes by so it's very quiet. I woke up in such a beautiful peace and felt His love very strongly.

It's a wonderful thing to be right with God and to have a clear conscience.

> Let us draw near with a true heart in full assurance of faith, with our hearts sprinkled clean from an evil conscience and our bodies washed with pure water. (Hebrews 10:22)

You see, Jesus sees right into your heart. You cannot hide from Him. If you think you can hide from Him, you are very mistaken. Take it from me, someone who thought she could hide her sins from the Almighty. My sins were many and He saw them all. However, His mercy was greater than all of my sins. It's very humbling to experience God's mercy. Here are a couple of lines from a song that resonate with me right now: "But I called on His name, in the dark of my shame, and His mercy was as gentle as silence."

> Blessed be the LORD! For he has heard the voice of my pleas for mercy. (Psalm 28:6)

I really thought I had gone so far away that I couldn't come back to Him. But no matter how far away from Him you travel, He knows where you are. He waits. He is just waiting for you to come back to Him. This is why the story of the prodigal son is in the Gospels. Jesus wanted everyone to know that we could return to Him no matter what we had done or how far away we were.

When the prodigal son returned, his father put on a feast for him because he was so happy to have his beloved son back. And it's the same with God: He rejoices when a wayward child comes back. Jesus illustrated this in the Parable of the Lost Coin.

> "Or what woman, having ten silver coins, if she loses one coin, does not light a lamp and sweep the house and seek diligently until she finds it? And when she has found it, she calls together her friends and neighbours, saying, 'Rejoice with me, for I have found the coin that I had lost.' Just so, I tell you, there is joy before the angels of God over one sinner who repents." (Luke 15: 8–10)

God will never reject a repentant heart.

> The sacrifices of God are a broken spirit; a broken and contrite heart, O God, you will not despise. (Psalm 51:17)

God doesn't keep beating you with a stick over your past sins. Once they are forgiven by Him, they are forgotten (Isaiah 43:25).

> He will again have compassion on us; he will tread our iniquities underfoot. You will cast all our sins into the depths of the sea. (Micah 7:19)

Lost Friendship; Distraction; The Lion of Judah; Pride

Monday, July 20

My sister and I drove to the garage to collect the tyre that was repaired and then had lunch at a nearby restaurant. It's been a beautiful day. We drove to a small beach and went farther on to a small village for a snack. It was like being on holidays!

A friend has bailed on me. She is ignoring me and clearly doesn't want to meet anymore. Friendship must be given freely, otherwise it's not a friendship in my eyes. If someone doesn't want to be friends anymore, I just let the person go and wish him or her well. It strikes me that some friendships may not survive the lockdowns.

Tuesday, July 21

This is my prayer this evening: Lord, be the beginning and end of my day. Comfort me in the days that lie ahead. Uncertainty and unemployment lie ahead, but I know I can rely on you, my Lord, to give me hope, courage and strength.

If I do anything today it will be to give thanks to Him.

> I will praise the name of God with a song; I will magnify him with thanksgiving. (Psalm 69:30)

It is so easy to be distracted away from Jesus. There are days when I fail; I become completely distracted and He isn't at the centre of my life. But I call out to Him again and say "Jesus, I'm here, help me to focus on You. I'm ready to listen. I give you my mind, body, soul, and spirit and I submit my will to you."

It's been a lovely sunny day. I went for a cycle, and then I walked the bike up this little walking trail that I hadn't walked before. I love discovering new places. I was able to put the current situation to the back of my mind and just enjoy the moment I was in. I love to hop on my bike and not think about anything much at all. I actually met a fellow cyclist and we cycled some of the way back together. I enjoyed having company.

Prayer time is not great tonight. I'm just not feeling God's presence or the Holy Spirit tonight. But I stay to give honour to the King. I can almost hear him say, "Don't rush away. Stay awhile."

I'm going to bed too late. Discipline is one of my weaknesses I'm afraid, but tomorrow is another day.

Wednesday, July 22

I had a very, very good day. I went to a shopping centre with a friend and bought some summer clothes. We had a coffee there and we went for a walk afterwards. These lines from the psalms struck me this evening. The heart of God is beautiful.

> For he delivers the needy when he calls, the poor and him who has no helper. He has pity on the weak and the needy, and saves the lives of the needy. From oppression and violence he redeems their life, and precious is their blood in his sight. (Psalm 72:12–14)

I consider myself poor in spirit and weak and in need of God's love and care every day.

I'm praying that God will open a door so that I can meet other believers and that we can worship freely.

Thursday, July 23

It's been another beautiful day. I met a friend for lunch. I feel very relaxed, calm, and happy even and, most of all, I feel very well. Here is a lovely extract from the psalms this evening.

> Oh, how abundant is your goodness, which you have stored up for those who fear you and worked for those who take refuge in you, in the sight of the children of mankind! In the cover of your presence you hide them from the plots of men; you store them in your shelter from the strife of tongues. (Psalm 31:19–20)

God is also called the Lion of Judah and He can roar with power. Here are some lines from a song.

> The Lord is a lion, the lion of Judah, He's roaring with power and fighting our battles. Every knee shall bow and every town confess that Jesus Christ is Lord. ("The Lion and the Lamb")

Lion

Sometimes I forget that Jesus is all powerful because He is God. He will also be a Judge but He is a just judge. As David Wilkerson said in one of his sermons, when Jesus returns, He will come with a sickle in His hand to separate the wheat from the chaff.

> Then I looked, and behold, a white cloud, and seated on the cloud one like a son of man, with a golden crown on his head, and a sharp sickle in his hand. (Revelation 14:14)

Remember His righteous anger when people held a market in the temple? He overturned tables and used a whip to hunt the animals and the people out.

Lord, keep me humble always. I think it's important to pray for humility. Humility, to me, means I recognise the power of God and my own wretchedness. Pride is deadly to the soul. When there's pride, you no longer think you need God in your life, and you can slowly start to drift away from Him. The soul begins to turn away.

> Do nothing from selfish ambition or conceit, but in humility count others more significant than yourselves. (Philippians 2:3)

> The reward for humility and fear of the Lord is riches and honour and life. (Proverbs 22:4)

"Be still and know that I am God", Childlike; "Do Not Let your Heart be Troubled"

Sunday July 26

This evening, I heard this in my spirit: "Be still and know that I am God."

Last week, I spent quite some time reading newspapers and watching the news. This morning, I felt the Holy Spirit say to "be more childlike." Jesus said that to inherit the kingdom of God, we must become like children. Children are innocent and trusting. They don't worry about tomorrow but are always in the present moment.

> At that time the disciples came to Jesus, saying, "Who is the greatest in the kingdom of heaven?" And calling to him a child, he put him in the midst of them and said, "Truly, I say to you, unless you turn and become

> like children, you will never enter the kingdom of heaven. Whoever humbles himself like this child is the greatest in the kingdom of heaven." (Mark 18:1–6)

I went for a cycle with my group last night. We did about thirty kilometres and will be meeting again on Saturday. I applied for three part-time jobs yesterday so that is positive. I will be applying for more today.

It's raining today—it's a soft, misty rain. I love this kind of rain. Silent rain.

I spent time with God this evening. I had neglected this time for a few days. How good He is that He reaches down to me and lifts me up. This is the psalm from this evening's prayer time.

> Not to us, O LORD, not to us, but to your name give glory, for the sake of your steadfast love and your faithfulness! (Psalm 115:1)

God's love is constant even when our love is not. He is faithful to us even when we are not. It's so good to feel His presence again and He imparts His peace to me once more. Thank you, Lord. I am without words.

I heard this in my spirit just now: "Do not let your heart be troubled."

Lord, let me place my full trust in You again, that I may have that childlike trust in You Lord that You take delight in. It is impossible to trust in God and be fearful at the same time.

If only people understood that believing in God is very liberating. He liberates you from fear of the future, from worry and anxiety, and He gives a joy and a peace that surpasses all understanding. It can only be found in Him. People search high and low for this peace and they don't find it.

PART III

Autumn 2020

God Knows our Thoughts; In the Palm of His Hands; Living in Limbo

Saturday, August 1

Even though August is the beginning of autumn, it's always considered a summer month in Ireland as the weather is as good as it would be in July, if not better sometimes.

Today, I went for a walk in a small woods that is near where I live. The air was cool and fresh, and I saw two red squirrels (which are native to Ireland). God knew my thoughts, as I was only thinking how I had never seen a red squirrel, and I was hoping to see one while I was in the woods. I was very close to the second one and I saw that he had a tiny white patch on his chest. It was fascinating to see how fast they moved.

The scriptures say that God discerns our thoughts from afar and knows all our ways.

A prodigal daughter

> O LORD, you have searched me and known me! You know when I sit down and when I rise up; you discern my thoughts from afar. You search out my path and my lying down and are acquainted with all my ways. (Psalm 139:1–4)

Squirrel

This is this evening's psalm reading.

> Out of my distress I called on the LORD; the LORD answered me and set me free. The LORD is on my side; I will not fear. What can man do to me? The LORD is on my side as my helper; I shall look in triumph on those who hate me.
>
> It is better to take refuge in the LORD than to trust in man. It is better to take refuge in the LORD than to trust in princes. (Psalm 118:5–9)

Thursday, August 6

I find that the days are going by quickly. All of this week, I have been waking up full of peace. You see how good the Lord Jesus is? He never forgets me but keeps blessing me.

I heard David Wilkerson say this in a short sermon I listened to yesterday: The sign of a person that trusts God is that they are at rest, and they don't have a worry in the world. I'm glad to say I feel that way at this moment in time. How priceless it is to not have a care in the world and to know that God himself has you in the palm of His hand.

> Behold, I have engraved you on the palms of my hands; your walls are continually before me. (Isaiah 49:16)

Sure, there are times I may feel restless and a little lacking in direction. I'm missing the company of friends and wonder when I will be working again. But I'm not anxious, worried, or upset. I know everything will work out. I'm trusting Jesus to find me a job and I know I will be working again soon. I don't doubt this for a second. I'm sleeping very deeply this week. Thank you, God, for sending me into a deep sleep.

The opening of the public houses is being postponed for three weeks. Public houses that serve food can open but public houses that just serve drinks are not open. They were supposed to open this week but it's not happening now.

Monday, August 10

The wearing of face coverings/masks in retail outlets, bars, and restaurants and public transport is now mandatory as of today.

Tuesday, August 11

I went for a cycle with my cycling group today. The pace was fast so it was a good challenge. I really enjoy the social aspect of the cycles. God didn't design us to be alone all of the time. It's not good for people's spirits or mental health.

I actually went to my church on Sunday. I was surprised at how small the congregation was. I guess some people are avoiding indoor gatherings still. There was no tea/coffee afterwards as would be usual and everyone disappeared quickly after the service.

Thursday, August 13

I miss having a job. I know I will have a job soon, I just don't know when.

> "Therefore I tell you, whatever you ask in prayer, believe that you have received it, and it will be yours."
> (Mark 11:24)

Sunday, August 16

I was at my family home again at the weekend and went for a swim. The water wasn't cold at all, and it was so refreshing. I want to create memories for this year, as there have been so many occasions cancelled and there is very little to remember the year by.

Life seems very strange without any social life at all. There are no gigs, no plays, and no concerts. We are all living in this limbo and much of life has been put on pause. It's quite frustrating living with restrictions.

Monday, August 17

Designated prayer time has become very important to me; it centres me again and reminds me to keep Jesus front and centre of my life.

Today, I set off on my bike at noon. I stopped off at a garage after about forty minutes and had a sandwich and coffee in a nearby park. I was back home at 3:00 p.m. It rained while I was out, and I quite like cycling in the rain as I find it refreshing.

Here are this evening's scriptures.

> For as high as the heavens are above the earth, so great is his steadfast love toward those who fear him; as far as the east is from the west, so far does he remove our transgressions from us.

As a father shows compassion to his children, so the LORD shows compassion to those who fear him. For he knows our frame; he remembers that we are dust. (Psalm 103:11–14)

But when the goodness and loving kindness of God our Savior appeared, he saved us, not because of works done by us in righteousness, but according to his own mercy, by the washing of regeneration and renewal of the Holy Spirit, whom he poured out on us richly through Jesus Christ our Savior, so that being justified by his grace we might become heirs according to the hope of eternal life. (Titus 3:4–7)

Friendship with Jesus; New Restrictions; His Father's House; A Veil

Tuesday, August 18

A good day! I was quite tired this morning after the cycle yesterday. I walked to the woods nearby again today. I left at 3:00 p.m. and was home at 5:00 p.m. I bumped into an acquaintance and a friend of hers on the way there and we stopped for a chat.

While in the woods, I diverted up into a small, secluded area and had a snack. I sat there for about twenty minutes and listened to the sounds around me. I sang a song of praise and talked to Jesus. I felt very renewed afterwards. God is amazing. It's amazing to think He hears me and enjoys spending time with me.

Human friendships take time and effort, and with Jesus, it's the same. We need to give Him our time and put the effort into developing a relationship with Him. How can you develop a relationship with anyone if you don't spend time with them?

Jesus considers *us* His friends. He said this to the apostles:-

> "No longer do I call you servants, for the servant does not know what his master is doing; but I have called you friends, for all that I have heard from my Father I have made known to you." (John 15:15)

To be considered a friend of Jesus is my greatest honour.

On the walk up to the woods, I was thinking about how much better life is when I keep it simple with God. I was saying to Him how I trust Him completely. From the moment I wake to the moment I fall asleep, He is on my mind and in my heart. I'm so glad I decided to make a conscious effort to spend time with Him every day and I've been richly rewarded. This is the wonderful thing about God: he rewards us so richly.

> Blessed is the man who remains steadfast under trial, for when he has stood the test he will receive the crown of life, which God has promised to those who love Him. (James 1:12)

As of today, new restrictions are in place until at least the thirteenth of September. Visitors allowed to your home are limited to six people from no more than three households. People over seventy are to limit their interactions and shop at the designated time. All outdoor gatherings and events are limited to fifteen people (reduced from 200). Indoor events are limited to six (reduced from fifty) except for businesses and shops. Restaurants and cafés must now close at 11:30 p.m. Summer camps are now limited to fifteen people. All sporting events are now behind closed doors (no spectators) and social gatherings before and after games are prohibited. Gyms are now reduced to a capacity of six people. Public transport is to be avoided if at all possible.

Wednesday, August 19

I was thinking of this just now while I was in prayer time:

> If you want hope,
>
> If you want love,
>
> If you want truth,
>
> Turn to God.

He will satisfy all of your needs. There is only one true God, and He is filling up my spirit right now.

Before I came down to pray, I was very despondent because of the new restrictions imposed yesterday. But now, I have hope in my heart and have joy and peace.

Nothing can ever take God away from me because His spirit dwells within me. This is the real treasure of being a child of God: wherever I go, He goes with me. He can reach you right in your own room. He will come to you. Just ask and you will receive all He wants to give you. He resides in us and He promises to make a place for us in His Father's house.

> "In my Father's house are many rooms. If it were not so, would I have told you that I go to prepare a place for you?" (John 14:2)

> For we know that if the tent that is our earthly home is destroyed, we have a building from God, a house not made with hands, eternal in the heavens. (2 Corinthians 5:1)

Sometimes, I find it hard to get my head around the fact that Jesus loves me so, so much. But it's a truth. I guess I will only really know how much when I get to see Him face to face. I'm not quite sure that humans could keep living in this world if they actually experienced His love in full. Maybe there is a veil there for our own good and this veil will only be lifted when we see Him face to face.

No Losers in God's Eyes; Birthday Party; The Broken Hearted

Sunday, August 23

It is easy to begin to think of yourself as a loser when you don't have a job. But there are no losers in God's eyes. God doesn't use the same measures the world uses. I think this is worth saying twice: in God's eyes, there are no losers.

God is for me; He is not against me. He is in the business of restoring people and not breaking them down.

> What then shall we say to these things? If God is for us, who can be against us? (Romans 8:31)

I was at a friend's house last night to celebrate her birthday with her family. it was a very enjoyable night and we had great fun singing karaoke.

Monday, August 24

My pet got knocked down at the weekend. I'm devastated he's gone. Loss is always hard, even if it's a pet. I got him just before everything was locked down and he had settled in well. He was looking really healthy and was becoming more confident in himself. I feel broken hearted that he's gone. What does God say about the broken-hearted?

A broken heart

He heals the broken hearted and binds up their wounds. (Psalm 147:3)

The LORD is near to the broken-hearted and saves the crushed in spirit. (Psalm 34:18)

Fear not, for I am with you; be not dismayed, for I am your God; I will strengthen you, I will help you, I will uphold you with my righteous right hand. (Isaiah 41:10)

Tuesday, August 25

I met with some friends at a hotel for lunch. It was very pleasant. I went for an hour's walk when I got back home. I noticed that the leaves have started falling. The sound of the wind through the tress was really loud and the sound reminded me of the power of God.

God is always with you in the storms of life if we turn to Him. Jesus, my constant companion, is walking me through this storm (lockdowns and so on).

Most Important Thing; The Sea; Division

Wednesday, August 26

The most important thing I now do every day is spend time in prayer. It can be so easy to brush this time aside as not important, but it is vital. If we don't spend this time with Him, how can He give us His joy and peace? I feel the stream of His life-giving water enrich me right now.

Thursday, August 27

I went to a nearby shopping centre this morning for a coffee and a slice of cake. Everyone was wearing face coverings in the centre and the atmosphere was flat and dead. All the joy has been sucked out of life. On a positive note, there are no deaths being reported at the moment.

I feel distracted and slightly despondent today as I'm missing my pet. I'm thinking of booking a surfing lesson. I'm going to the beach tomorrow. I checked the forecast and big swells are forecasted. I can't wait to get into the water. The sea doesn't care how you're feeling; it just does its thing!

I spent a long time on the computer today applying for jobs. I applied for a job in my area that I'm hoping to get. It involves working with children. This will be a change of career but it's an area I have wanted to work in for a while. This just may be the opportunity I've been waiting for. I had applied to work with children before but wasn't successful as I don't have a lot of experience. *If at first you don't succeed, try, try again!*

Saturday, August 29

I went to the beach yesterday and, as forecasted, the waves were huge. I didn't do much swimming as the waves were coming so quick and fast, I couldn't swim. The waves were so strong that I was propelled back onto the shore, and at one point, I was completely submerged under a wave for a couple of seconds.

There, in the ocean, I felt God so close at hand and praised Him for His creation.

Monday, August 31

I notice more and more people are wearing face coverings, even walking on the streets outside. I went into a camera shop to get some photos printed out. The person behind the counter wasn't wearing a face covering and it was uplifting to have someone in a shop smile back at me.

The lockdowns have begun to divide people. We are indeed in unprecedented times.

Tuesday, September 1

I'm down in the dumps today and haven't felt like this in quite a while. I try not to indulge in self-pity but take heart that the God of heaven loves me and He has angels at both sides of me.

> For he will command his angels concerning you to guard you in all your ways. (Psalm 91:11)

The isolation and lack of social interaction is taking a toll on me. It's very difficult not to be affected by it. There is nothing to look forward to.

Tuesday, September 8

I'm back! I hadn't felt like writing at all. I had been waking up at around four o'clock in the morning all of last week, and thankfully, I slept well last night. I think the stress of the last five months has hit me like a wrecking ball.

I realise I need to make more of an effort to meet up with people. I am putting more of a structure on my days now and I'm sticking to a timetable. I'm making plans to meet up with people rather than waiting for them to contact me.

I had a surfing lesson on Saturday just past and thoroughly enjoyed it. I stood up on the board a few times and managed to stay on for a few seconds. I found the lesson boosted my spirits.

I will get a part-time job soon. It's always important to be able to see an end in sight. It's just a matter of time before I'm working again.

Thursday, September 10

I have been feeling overwhelmed by my current situation and I take heart from this scripture that I read this morning.

> When I thought, "My foot slips," your steadfast love, O LORD, held me up. (Psalm 94:18)

Good News; Old Acquaintances; Passing Through

Wednesday, September 30

I have been offered the job working with children that I wanted. I'm so thrilled and relieved! The start date is not yet confirmed, but it will be soon.

Sunday, October 4

It is October already! I went to a small Christian church service in my area this morning. It's a lively, friendly group of believers. I knew a few in attendance as old acquaintances. It was so enjoyable to be singing and praising God with no hindrances. Everyone was so friendly and happy. I had a long chat with my very old acquaintance and we exchanged numbers.

I am thankful that I can go to this church in my area. I really want to grow in my faith life and bear fruit. My fear is that I would become lukewarm from not going to a church regularly.

Saturday, October 10

A good day—fresh and bright. I went on a long walk and had a few conversations with people along the way. I try to strike up conversations with people as often as I can.

When I came back, I had a toasted sandwich. I watched a film at around four o'clock called *Elsewhere*. It was funny in parts and was set in Canada. The scenery was amazing. It was good to switch off from everything and enjoy a film. I find that time is beginning to move quicker.

I have felt the companionship of Jesus all day today and I wonder what it would be like to be in His actual real presence in heaven. I do find the concept of eternity difficult to grasp—the concept of forever and ever. In paradise, this earthly life will hardly be remembered. I think the only regret would be that I didn't spend more time with Him while on earth.

I do believe we are passing through this life. The scriptures say our lives are like passing shadows.

> Man is like a breath; his days are like a passing shadow (Psalm 144:4)

We do not know what tomorrow will bring and a person is like a mist that appears and vanishes. These are sobering words.

> Come now, you who say, "Today or tomorrow we will go into such and such a town and spent a year there and trade and make a profit"—yet you do not know what tomorrow will bring. What is your life? For you are a mist that appears for a little time and then vanishes. (James 4:13—14)

Sunday, October 11

It was a beautiful autumn day today—it's my favourite season.

I drove to the place where the church was meeting last week but they weren't there and I was so disappointed. The joy and happiness in the room last Sunday was such a contrast to our everyday lives right now. I wonder why they weren't there. It might have something to do with regulations. I don't know.

My sister and I went to an open-air market afterwards. Lots of people were wearing masks outdoors. People are feeling fearful.

I haven't got a start date for my job yet as there are some formalities that have to be completed. I assume it will be soon though and I will bide my time between now and then.

I'm a bit worried about Ireland moving into Level 5 restrictions which I feel may be on the horizon. The government are saying they may have to impose them again. Everything is up in the air and we are living with a lot of uncertainty.

Level 5 Restrictions; Fearless; Setting the Captives Free

Monday, October 19

I began my job on the thirteenth of October and am very grateful to be working again.

The entire country is going back to Level 5 restrictions from midnight on 21 October until the first of December. There are rising cases, but thankfully no deaths at the moment. My place of work is considered an essential service so I will still be going to work every day (even if the schools are closed).

I called out to my friend's house (who had the birthday party) after work and it was lovely visit, as always. We wanted to meet before the restrictions were in place.

Sunday, October 25

Today, I have a childlike joy. Thank you, my Lord, for imparting Your joy to me and for taking away my fear.

> You will not fear the terror of the night, nor the arrow that flies by day, nor the pestilence that stalks in darkness, nor the destruction that wastes at noonday. (Psalm 91:5–6)

People can be prisoners in their minds and can be bound by fear and anxieties. The good news is that Jesus came to set the captives free. This is the scripture He read in the synagogue at the very beginning of His ministry.

> And he came to Nazareth, where he had been brought up. And as was his custom, he went to the synagogue on the Sabbath day, and he stood up to read. And the scroll of the prophet Isaiah was given to him. He unrolled the scroll and found the place where it was written,

> "The Spirit of the Lord is upon me, because he has anointed me to proclaim good news to the poor. He has sent me to proclaim liberty to the captives and recovering of sight to the blind, to set at liberty those who are oppressed, to proclaim the year of the Lord's favour." (Luke 4:16–19)

If only people knew how God raises up the lowly and pours out His spirit to comfort them.

Drabness; New Garments in Heaven

Monday, October 26 (bank holiday weekend)

What a strange time we are in! I want to wake up from this bad dream (lockdown). My sister and I drove to a nearby beach for a short visit. People were in swimming and one man said the water was warm. We didn't meet any checkpoints on the journey.

Saturday, October 31

It's hard to believe we are back to where we started at Level 5 lockdown. Now, it is only items deemed essential that can be bought in the shops and parents can't buy clothes or shoes for their children. They must be purchased online or by click and collect.

There must be so many under severe stress: people with mortgages who are worried about job losses; parents worried about their children missing school; business owners worried their business will close for good; and nursing home residents who are denied visits from their loved ones. I think of those who are suffering with the virus in hospital and it must be scary for them.

I take comfort in knowing that nothing can separate me from God's love. Paul, the apostle said this:-

> For I am sure that neither death nor life, nor angels nor rulers, nor things present nor things to come, nor powers, nor height nor depth, nor anything else in all creation, will be able to separate us from the love of God in Christ Jesus our Lord. (Romans 8:38–39)

PART IV

Winter 2020/2021

Restrictions Ahead

Sunday, November 1

It's officially winter! Today seems like a very, very long day. It's been raining all day long. I have no news at all, but God's love is imprinted on my heart like a seal.

Thursday, November 19

I feel I need to detach myself from it all (lockdown, etc.) and put my focus solely on Jesus and on my spiritual life. Today, I prayed for health and vitality in my mind and body. Life is not enjoyable right now, but in Jesus, I find gladness.

> The meek shall obtain fresh joy in the Lord, and the poor among mankind shall exult in the Holy One of Israel. (Isaiah 29:19)

> For you, O Lord, have made me glad by your work; at the works of your hands I sing for joy. (Psalm 92:4)

Tuesday, November 24

Our Tánaiste (vice-president) Leo Varadkar has announced that a third wave of restrictions may be required in the new year. Things aren't looking very good.

Friday, November 27

It was announced today that we would be moving to Level 3 on the first of December. This means that all non-essential retail shops, hair salons, gyms, leisure centres, cinemas, museums, galleries, religious buildings, and places of worship can reopen. Churches must restrict their congregation to fifty people. Schools and adult education facilities can also open. Restaurants and cafés can open for takeaway and delivery. People can dine outdoors (maximum fifteen people). You can have visitors to you home but only from one other household (maximum six people).

People have been asked to stay in their regions and to keep the number of people they meet to a minimum.

Thursday, December 3

What kind of Christmas is in store for us this year I wonder?

In prayer time this morning, I felt the Holy Spirit pour out His love and peace on me. He illuminated my mind and my spirit soared again. I asked Him to renew my spirit and set my heart on fire for Jesus as I feel like I've been walking in mud recently, weighed down by the isolation and restrictions.

I heard this in my spirit: that God will give us new garments in heaven.

> The one who conquers will be clothed thus in white garments, and I will never blot his name out of the book of life. I will confess his name before my Father and before his angels. (Revelation 3:5)

I hope I will be among those who conquer.

Jesus: Man of Sorrows; A "Sharp Lockdown"

Friday, December 4

I drove into town to drop my car to a garage and went to a café for a coffee and cake. It was enjoyable to experience normality again. I feel a huge sense of relief that Level 5 has been lifted for now. I expect a sharp, hard lockdown in January as our government has more or less said that this will happen, but I rely on God to see me through.

> He gives power to the faint, and to him who has no might he increases strength. (Isaiah 40:29)

Jesus doesn't dismiss our sufferings and He identifies with us in our despair. The prophet Isaiah described Jesus as "a man of sorrows" who was rejected by men and familiar with grief. He was despised and held in low esteem.

> He was despised and rejected by men, a man of sorrows and acquainted with grief; and as one from whom men hide their faces he was despised, and we esteemed him not. (Isaiah 53:3)

Friday, December 11

Today, I did some house cleaning and decluttering after work. It was a good distraction.

A New Year; House Meetings; Christmas 2020

Tuesday, January 2

We were thankful that we could travel home for Christmas and we had a nice Christmas.

Wednesday, January 3

As anticipated, Ireland is now in its third Level 5 lockdown, which will remain in place until January 12. Pubs, restaurants, and hair salons have been closed since Christmas Eve. It really doesn't feel like a new year.

I love this psalm and it lifts my spirits.

> Satisfy us in the morning with your steadfast love, that we may rejoice and be glad all our days. (Psalm 90:14)

I have been regularly attending a house prayer meeting, which is attended by a very small number of people, since October. It is being held by the acquaintance I met last July and I know of a few other small groups who are also gathering in homes to worship God.

Our government introduced fines for breaches of the guidelines in November. Organisers of an event, inside or outside a private dwelling, can be fined 500 euros and anyone attending can be fined 150 euros. Anyone breaching the travel restrictions can be fined 100 euros.

I had a choice to make: attend the meetings and risk the consequences or stay at home. I choose to go because my relationship with God is everything to me. I have benefited greatly from attending. We sing worship songs, read from the Bible, and have communion. We then stay for tea/coffee and chat afterwards.

Friday, January 15

Prayer time has become something I do daily now without much struggle. It's almost like I hear Jesus calling me. I feel a pull in my heart to go and spend time alone with Him. I seek Him in that secret place and I find Him.

I'm praying/talking more with the Holy Spirit these days. He is the consoler and the comforter.

> And I will ask the Father, and he will give you another Helper, to be with you forever, even the Spirit of truth, whom the world cannot receive, because it neither sees him nor knows him. You know him, for he dwells with you and will be in you. (John 14:16–17)

His Healing Hand upon Me; Green Pastures

Sunday, January 17

We had a house meeting yesterday morning, and the Lord touched me in a very profound way. I heard these words in my spirit: "My healing hand is upon you" and the experience was so, so beautiful. I was enveloped in the unconditional, all powerful love of God. There is no mistaking the touch of His hand! It was as if He was standing right in front of me and I could have reached out and touched Him.

I'm thinking of the woman who only touched the hem of the garment Jesus was wearing and was instantly healed because she believed in Him.

> She had heard the reports about Jesus and came up behind Him and touched his garment. For she said "If I touch even his garments, I will be made well" and immediately, the flow of blood dried up and she felt in her body that she was healed of her disease. (Mark 5:27–29)

There's a hymn I know that describes what I mean: "He touched me, He touched me and oh the joy that filled my soul. Something happened, now I know, He touched me and made me whole."

The prophet Isaiah said that by His wounds we are healed.

> But he was pierced for our transgressions; he was crushed for our iniquities; upon him was the chastisement that brought us peace, and with his wounds we are healed. (Isaiah 53:5)

Every blow He received, and every hammer of the nails into His hands and feet brought healing today. Saying "thank you" sounds so inadequate.

I am here giving thanks to Him. This is my prayer tonight: Thank you, thank you Jesus, for what you have done for me, my Lord and my God. I cannot put my gratitude into words.

Wednesday, January 20

Jesus, the Good Shepherd, has truly brought me to green pastures and led me beside still waters. He has walked me through the lockdowns.

Being His Friend; The Way; My Treasure

Thursday, January 21

Even though the days are passing by quickly, the month seems long. January always seems long but with the lockdown, it seems even longer than usual. I am thankful to be feeling healthy, well, and content.

I had to write down this psalm I read this evening because it's so beautiful.

> The friendship of the LORD is for those who fear him, and he makes known to them his covenant. My eyes are ever towards the LORD for He will pluck my feet out of the net. (Psalm 25:14–15)

People can forget about you, but Jesus never forgets. He is completely loyal and trustworthy.

Friday, January 22

There will be no easing of restrictions at the end of January, but, I am content and unafraid and this is God's blessing for sure. I live one day at a time and appreciate the ordinary, everyday things. Today, my heart is so overflowing with joy and peace.

You know, being a follower of Jesus is exciting. Knowing Him is exciting. Many may attempt to show a way, but it is bound to lead to unfulfillment and disillusion. Jesus said that He is the way, the truth, and the life.

> Thomas said to him, "Lord, we do not know where you are going. How can we know the way?" Jesus said to him, "I am the way, and the truth, and the life. No one comes to the Father except through me." (John 14:5–7)

Arrow

If you have ever found yourself lost on a journey, you can become frantic to know the way to your destination. How relieved you are when you are back on the right road! God will not lead you astray or bring confusion into your life; instead, He brings clarity and certainty to your life, and you will never be lost again.

I would not trade my life with Him for anything or anyone. You could offer me a million pounds and I would say no.

Thursday, January 28

I am experiencing His presence more and more and I so desire it. I just opened the psalms on this page and it perfectly matches my sentiments this evening.

> For God alone, O my soul, wait in silence, for my hope is from him. He only is my rock and my salvation, my fortress; I shall not be shaken. On God rests my salvation and my glory; my mighty rock, my refuge is God.
>
> Trust in him at all times, O people; pour out your heart before him; God is a refuge for us. (Psalm 62:5–8)

PART V

Spring 2021

Springtime; The Best Years; Trusting in Others; Simplicity; The Best Part of my Day

Monday, February 1

It's springtime at last! It feels like it's been a long wait to get to the first day of spring!

I have felt God has been with me all day and there is such joy in my heart.

My heart is dancing with happiness. Songs of praise escape my lips. I can't hold them in.

When I look back on my life, I see that the years when I followed Him were the most fulfilling years. I realise that when I chose to live outside of His ways and live a sinful life, I immediately became cut off from Him and His Holy Spirit fled my life right there and then.

A prodigal daughter

When I didn't have God in my life, I put my trust in others: family, friends, boyfriends, and work colleagues. Human nature, being what it is, ultimately makes trusting in others precarious and disappointing because no one is perfect and all are flawed. Only God is wholly trustworthy.

My writings about my walk with God are not complicated and are somewhat childlike at times. But we actually become like children again when we know God. I live my faith in a very simplistic way. It's not highbrow or intellectual. I talk with Him. I sing songs of praise and I give Him thanks and read the scriptures. My prayer time can sometimes be twenty minutes, forty minutes, or an hour, sometimes more than an hour, and it's the best part of my day.

Epilogue

Ireland's Level 5 lockdown remained in place until the twelfth of April 2021.

There were fewer restrictions in place after April and Ireland never went back to Level 5. All restrictions were lifted in January 2022 (except for masks to be worn on public transport and in most public spaces).

My sister, whom I live with, became a believer in June of 2021. The believers who hosted the meeting had a visit from the police on a Sunday morning in March, 2021 and so the meetings had to cease.

I began to host the meetings in my home six weeks later with the agreement of my sister. She joined us in the meetings and, over time, gave her life to Jesus. It was wonderful to see her become a believer and see how Jesus is changing her life for the better. When she stands beside me in worship together in our home, I am in awe of what God has done for her.

God was still at work despite the churches being closed. You see, God is not confined to the walls of any building because He is Spirit. The Holy Spirit is like the wind and blows where it wishes. Can anyone stop the wind?

> The wind blows where it wishes, and you hear its sound, but you do not know where it comes from or where it goes. So it is with everyone who is born of the Spirit. (John 3:8)

Bibliography

Central Christian Church. "The Crucifixion: A Medical Perspective." YouTube video. 28 March 2008. https://www.youtube.com/watch?v=T-EVfxABSoU.

"Hematidrosis." Segen's Medical Dictionary. Accessed 19 October 2022. https://medical-dictionary.thefreedictionary.com/hematidrosis.

"Medical Description of the Flogging and Crucifixion of Jesus." Bible Studies for Skeptics, Seekers, and Believers. Accessed: 20 June 2020. https://bsssb-llc.com/medical-description-of-the-flogging-and-crucifixion-of-jesus/.

"Why did they break the legs of the men that were crucified with Jesus?" Answers from the Book. Accessed: 22 June 2020. http://answersfromthebook.net/why-did-they-break-the-legs-of-the-men-that-were-crucified-with-jesus/.

https://www.gov.ie/en/speech/72f0d9-national-address-by-the-taoiseach-st-patricks-day/ Accessed: 17 March 2020

https://www.gov.ie/en/publication/b07ffe-reopening-business-elements/ Accessed: 18 May 2020

https://www.irishtimes.com/news/crime-and-law/covid-19-fines-system-expected-to-come-into-force-this-week-1.4399265 Accessed: 21 November 2020

Ingram Content Group UK Ltd.
Milton Keynes UK
UKHW042035270423
420913UK00002B/21